Political Theology in Transition

Political Theology in Transition

Y. T. Vinayaraj

Christian World Imprints

First Published in 2020 by

Christian World Imprints
Christian Publishing & Books from India
C-3, Wazirpur Industrial Area
Delhi-110052
cwidelhi2017@gmail.com
www.ChristianWorldImprints.com
Phone: +91 11 41526079

ISBN: 978-93-5148-500-1 (HB)
ISBN: 978-93-5148-501-8 (PB)

Printed in India.

Contents

Foreword

Y. T. Vinayaraj is one of the few Asian theologians for whom theology is a constant struggle. Despite the general belief that the so-called liberation theology has now more or less come to an end, he continues to see in it a means of thinking through some of the most important issues and problems of contemporary church and society. In this profoundly engaging book, he calls for a church of the multitude, a church without sovereignty - an open network in which all differences can be expressed freely and equally and a platform of hospitality where no one is excluded.

Forty five years ago Paul Lehmann bemoaned the widening gap between biblical and revolutionary politics and called for the transfiguration of politics in response to an environment of growing conflict and violence around issues of racism, capitalism and imperialism. His call was accompanied by a survey of the theory and practice of revolutionaries from Marx to Mao and Ho Chi Minh; from Fidel and Che Guevara to Camillo Torres and Nestor Paz Zamora; from Frantz Fanon to Martin Luther King, Jr., Malcom X, and the Black Panther Party. He wanted political revolutions to reconsider the question of violence and become more spiritual by turning toward the ideals of Jesus. However, his line of thinking seems to be that much must be said on both sides. While reproaching revolutionary politics for its rabid materialism, he overlooked the fact that his own magisterial authority derived from an alliance of the politics of established power and the anti-revolutionary ideology of the church.

Unlike *The Transfiguration of Politics*, this book is produced on a different terrain. While Paul Lehmann practiced theology during the time of old imperialism which extended the sovereignty of European nations beyond their very borders with an inside and an outside, the work of Vinayaraj takes place in the context of what Hardt and Negri call Empire, the name they have given to the political form of globalization. Unlike old imperialism, Empire has no borders, no centre, and no limits. 'It is a decentred and deterritorialized apparatus of rule that progressively incorporates the whole globe.' This does not mean that the sovereignty of nation states has vanished. We live in a period in which the victory of global capitalism and the defeat of any political alternative to neo-liberalism seem somewhat assured. It is also a period when global as well as national conflicts seem increasingly driven by faith-based politics.

In more and more countries those on the political right are questioning the separation between church/religion and state. Theological imperatives gain more space in the rhetoric of many contemporary political leaders. George W. Bush's description of 'war on terror' as a 'crusade' is an example. In order to cover up the contradictions marring the coherent identity of the nation, politicians are turning to the politics of good and evil. They depict secular politics as the battleground of good and evil. The politics of eschatology is also played out against progressive secular politics.

Any attempt toward a theology and ethics of responsible involvement in social change should take all these into account, especially, the challenges of both national politics and the politics of globalization. Vinayaraj is well aware of this and he makes his points with admirable clarity. At a time when theory is being continuously marginalized, he draws on theories and methodologies of contemporary cultural studies and postcolonial studies for help in reflecting on the possibility of a radical political theology. Recruiting resources from Spivak's notion of subalternity, Hardt and Negri's ideas of Empire and multitude, M. M. Thomas's theology of the cross, Agamben's reflections on the coming community, Ambedkar's contest against Brahmanical hierarchy, and Deleuz's idea of 'society of control', he is exploring the possibility for theology to connect with movements for a radical democracy.

The task of theology, in accordance with Spivak's notion of subalternity as 'a third position of being human other than the self and the other', is 'not to speak for the margin', rather, 'to learn to listen to the unspoken voices of the margin', and consider 'the subaltern as teacher.' This book of Vinayaraj invites us to share this insight and, like Spivak, provokes us to attempt to change 'conditions of impossibility – the hopeless and negative feeling that nothing will change for the disenfranchised – into a condition of possibility.'

T. M. Yesudasan

Acknowledgement

I would like to thank Prof. T. M. Yesudasan, former Professor, Department of English, CMS College, Kottayam for writing the foreword to this book; Indu Mary Yesudasan, Asst. Professor, Department of English, GPM Government College, Manjeshwaram for correcting the manuscript; Anshul Kanda, the editorial head, Christian World Imprints for publishing this book, and the staff and students of Mar Thoma Theological Seminary, Kottayam for all their support and encouragement.

Introduction

Any renewal of political order requires a renewal of theology.
John D. Caputo and Catherine Keller (2007:108)

There is no such thing as an un-political theology.
Jurgen Moltmann (2013:2)

If democracy is to be truly relevant in the face of global relationships, our concept and practice of democracy must make a giant leap forward. We must democratize democracy.
Jean-Betrant Aristide (2000:10)

Political philosophy and Christian theology in the Western tradition have always had a "strange alchemy" in between and thus, as John D. Caputo and Catherine Keller contend, any renewal of political thinking demands the renewal of Christian theology.[1] The partnership between political philosophy and Christian theology in the Western tradition in promoting the modern notions of sovereign state and democracy has already been exposed by the contemporary post-Continental political thinkers. Giorgio Agamben, the well-known Italian political philosopher and theologian categorically exposes the correlation between the Western concept of sovereign state and the ancient patristic theology of divine sovereignty.[2] This correlation was further legitimized by the Hobbesian (Thomas Hobbes) political philosophy and the Schmittian (Carl Schmitt) political theology in the modern period. When Johann Baptist Metz and Jurgen Moltmann envisioned a new turn in political theology in the form of a Liberation Theology in the Post-Auschwitz German context, they reclaimed the political content of Christian faith, but never addressed the inherent compromise on the notion of sovereignty. The post-Continental political thinkers such as Michael Hardt, Antonio Negri, Giorgio Agamben, Gilles Deleuze, Slavoj Zizek, Alain Badiou, and Catherine Malabou problematise the legitimisation of sovereignty in the Continental (postmodern) political theology and provoke Christian theology to take a radical turn towards new materialism.[3] This book tries to engage with those contemporary political philosophies in order to envisage a radical political theology in the immediate context of neoempire.

Political Theology in Transition

Political theology addresses the questions such as, the relationship between theology and politics; the relationship between church and state; the role of religion in public life; and to what extend religious belief should shape our political discourses. Though it seems like a "strange alchemy between oil and water" (Alistair Kee), theology and politics have had a complex and contestatory alliance in history.[4] The concept of 'political theology' connotes, as Jan Assmann suggests, the 'ever changing relationships between political community and religious order, in short, between power [or authority: *Herrschaft*] and salvation [*Heil*].[5] Historically, the term political theology dates Marcus Terentius Varro (116-27 BC) who speaks of the stoic tripartition of theology, in which a political theology is juxtaposed with mythical and cosmological theologies.

In the *City of God*, Augustine contrasts the divine city with an earthly city and refuses to sacralize the Roman Empire. However, the conversion of Constantine into Christianity turned up the whole situation upside down and thus opened up a new alliance between the empire and the church. In the medieval period we see the worst impact of the Christendom theology of the ancient church which leads it to the crusades and conflicts. Martin Luther in the reformation period re-signified the Augustinian theology of two kingdoms to challenge the illegitimate relationship between the church and the empire through papacy. It was the *Treaty of Westphalia* (1648) that marked the collapse of Christendom and gave secular authorities the power to determine matters of religion in their own state. When it comes to the enlightenment period, religion was relegated to a private space and there established a dichotomous relationship between theology and politics.

Political theology in the modern expression began with the emergence of German nationalism in 1920s and 1930s. As a response to the Nazi Governance, it was Carl Schmitt the German professor of constitutional law who initiated a modern discourse on political theology. It was the full expression of the political theology of the civil religion which was initiated by Machiavelli and Hobbes. Carl Schmitt's political theology was a eulogy of German nationalism which encouraged the German Christians in their legitimization of Hitler. Schmitt's political theology was a theology of divine sovereignty. Schmitt argued that "all signified concepts of the modern theory of the state are secularized theological concepts."[6] According to Schmitt, the "sovereign is he who decides on the state of exception."[7] Schmitt defended the dictatorship of Hitler in 1933 as a legitimate act of political sovereignty. Signifying the Christian eschatological thinking, Schmitt argued that the secular history is the realm of the battle between good and evil, friend and foe, God and Satan, state and anarchy. He believed that the reason for the delay of *parousia* of Christ is the legitimate time of *katechon* (2 Thess. 2:7)—the evil suppressing sovereign state. The role of the sovereign state is to restrain evil—the political anarchy—from the society. Jurgen Moltmann is extremely right when he finds connection between Schmitt's political theology and the contemporary US' theology of War on Terror.'[8]

Liberation Theologies: A New Turn in Political Theology

A new turn in political theology was offered by Johann Baptist Metz, the West German Roman Catholic theologian and Jurgen Moltmann, the Reformed theologian in 1960s in the post World War and post-Auschwitz German context. They envisioned a critical theology and responsible Christianity that reclaim the radical political content of Christian faith. The declarations of the Vatican II (1962-65) and the resurgence of the Lutheran reformation traditions influenced them in content and practice of a political-liberation theology. Johann B. Metz, in his *theology of the World*, emphasized the critical function of theology to "de-privatize Christianity" and to awake the church to "face the world."[9] Alluding to Marx, Metz offered a sharp critique of the traditional "other-worldly" theology which un-politicized Christian faith.[10] For Metz, Christian faith is not dogmatized but action oriented. Thus, he offered "orthopraxis" as the methodology of the political theology instead of "orthodoxy." As Jurgen Moltmann rightly highlights, it was Metz' inclination to Marxism helped him to develop a social theory of religious criticism and to envisage a praxiological methodology.[11]

Jürgen Moltmann upheld the view that "there is no such thing as an un-political theology."[12] One of the key aspects of his challenge to political theology is one of "speaking up" which he articulates it as the prophetic role of political theology. In that sense, Moltmann finds no distinction between political theology and liberation theology. Moltmann's political theology is also furnished with an eschatological sensibility through which he defined it as the theology of hope. His eschatological Christology—"Jesus—anticipator of the kingdom of God offered a glimpses of a political Christology which finds its full expression in his book *The Crucified God*. For Moltmann, "faith in the crucified Christ is in the political sense a public testimony to the freedom of Christ and the law of grace in the face of the political religions of nations, empires, races and classes."[13] Moltmann and Metz are to be acknowledged for their contributions to political theology in the frame of liberation theology. However, they never tried to address the inherent correlation between the sovereign state and the divine sovereignty in the Western tradition which invites interrogations form the post-continental philosophers and theologians.[14]

The religious criticism of the neo-Marxism of Ernst Bloch and the sharp social criticism of the Frankfurt School of Max Horkheimer, Theodor W. Adorno, Herbert Marcuse, Walter Benjamin and Jurgen Habermas accentuated the emergence of liberation theologies not only in Germany but also in Latin America, North America, and Asia that paved the way for the opening of political theology to the other parts of the world. The theologians like Gustavo Gutierrez, Leonardo Boff, Juan Luis Segundo, Jon Sobrino, Jose Porfirio Miranda offered a socio-economic hermeneutics in Latin America to initiate the struggle against capitalism and European colonialism. For the Church, it was a paradigm shift from its Christendom mentality to the solidarity mentality. Political theology in North America appeared in the form of Black liberation theology, Feminist theology, Hispanic theologies, and Asian American theology in 1970s. Black liberation movement initiated by Martin Luther King Jr. and Malcolm X invoked encouraged theologians like James H. Cone and Dwight Hopkins to think about Back theology and Black church. Asian liberation theologies like Minjung theology and Dalit theology brought the pathos of the marginalized sections in the south that further extended the canvas of the global contextual theology. Bringing feminist theology as her location, Elisabeth Schussler Fiorenza, on the other hand, added a postcolonial sensibility to political theology. She named it as the 'decolonizing political theology of liberation.'[15]

Radical Orthodoxy: A Postmodern Turn in Political Theology

Critiquing the liberation theology model, radical orthodoxy offered a postmodern turn in political theology in 1990s. Radical orthodoxy was initiated by the British Cambridge University theologians John Milbank, Catherine Pickstoke and Graham Ward. It was further continued by Rowan Williams, Fergus Kerr, Nicolas Lash, Stanly Hauerwas, David Burrell, and Peter Ochs. For the radical orthodoxy theologians, the modern notion of state and the whole project of modernity out of which the modern liberal democracy has emerged is a deviation. Radical orthodoxy signifies the postmodern critique of modernity and liberalism. It is closely linked with the postliberal theology initiated by Hans Frei and George Lindbeck. Postliberal theologians take the lead from Karl Barth who resists the correlationist habits of modern theology. In the same vein of thought,

John Milbank argues that "modernity is not a space of freedom and liberty, but it is the territory of new lord and master with a new discipline."[16] For him, in modern state, modern individuals are freed from the church and enslaved in the ontology of the liberal state.

To the radical orthodox theologians, the modern state is nothing but a new ontology of enslavement. Modern state and its social theories create conflicts, violence, and anarchy. On the other hand, radical orthodoxy substitutes God for the state in its role as the absolute mediator. God for the radical orthodoxy theologians is the sovereign God of the ancient Christendom who holds the overarching power over both the secular and the sacred world.[17] It is the omnipotent and the omniscient God who hold the absolute power and authority over the entire realm of human life. The transcendence of God includes the social and the political. Thus, for them, political is always theological. Radical orthodoxy's theology of transcendence/sovereignty does not allow any division between secular and sacred, theological and political. It takes us to the pre-modern Christian era where the Christendom mentality was prevailed. As Clayton Crocket contends, radical orthodoxy is based on the medieval vision of Christian empire that eliminates democracy as a viable political form of liberalism.[18]

Radical orthodoxy advises the modern liberal individuals to return to the pre-modern ethos and acknowledge the primacy and the authority of the Church which is of course not an institution but a divine community. Ecclesia, for the radical orthodoxy theologians, is a new sort of universal polity.[19] Graham Ward in his book *Christ and Culture* invokes us to submit to Christ rather than the modern state; because the authority of Christ substitutes for the power and the authority of the state.[20] For radical orthodoxy, all material realities are vehicles of grace and capable of disclosing transcendence. Material is in a state of "suspended transcendence." Politics is nothing but a "suspended transcendence." It is the role of theology to "super naturalize the natural/the political." According to the radical orthodoxy theologians God is the better sovereignty than the state. Only God can offer transcendence to the natural, the material, and the political. As Clayton Crocket contends, this is a much idealized notion of the medieval Christianity which is petitioned as an alternative to the modern and postmodern liberal politics and capitalism.[21] The problem with this political theology is that it fixes the state in its antagonism with Christianity and the church and legitimizes the authority of Church over the state, theology over the politics, sacred over the secular. As Kwok Pui-lan argues, radical orthodoxy legitimizes the European-colonial theological propaganda over the rest of the world.[22]

Critiquing liberation theology, Milbank in his book *Theology and Social Theory: Beyond Secular Reason* argues that liberation theology reduces divine salvation as a social activity. For him, liberation theory reduces transcendence as a social entity—"naturalizing the Supernatural" which is nothing but the crucial failure of modernity. Social theory has no separate identity and it is only an explanation of the religious experience. Social theory is originated from the theological knowledge and thus it has only a quasi religious status. Social logic or political thinking is just an illumination of the metaphysical thinking. Thus, what is social is incomplete and irrational in itself and always connected to the logic beyond it (Transcendental Thomism). Milbank argues that liberation theologians commit the mistake of 'socializing the transcendental' by reducing religious truth as mere social facts. For Milbank, what is political and social is already illuminating of the theological and thus, the final salvation should come from beyond—the sovereign God. Milbank's notion of transcendence is all-encompassing of all secular-political spaces and imaginations. In sum, radical orthodoxy, by critiquing the sovereignty of the modern state and the liberal capitalism, exhorts us to accept the power and authority of the Church and Christendom. In this sense, radical orthodoxy becomes yet another form of fundamentalism despite its criticisms of liberal economy and culture.[23]

"God without Sovereignty": Continental Political Theology in Transition

At around same time that radical orthodoxy was emerging upon the theological scene, a Continental philosophy of religion as taking place, influenced by the works of Derrida, Emmanuel Levinas and

Jean Luc Marion. This team of continental philosophy initiated a critical analysis of the Western notion of sovereignty and offered a de-ontological phase. Engaging with the Heideggerian critique of the Western monistic ontology, Levinas locates transcendence as exteriority.[24] Levinasian philosophy of the other replaced transcendence at the face of the other. Marion defined sovereignty of God as mystery or bedazzlement.[25] Both of them offered a sharp critique of the Western monotheistic tradition, but never discontinued the notion of the being which is closely linked with the identity of the West. Alluding to Judith Butler, Mayra Rivera argues that Levinas constitutes two types of beings: beings and alien beings where alien beings are considered as transcendent. Both Levinas and Marion retain transcendence as the focal point of ontology.[26]

In *Rogues*, Derrida traces back to the Western Christian monotheism to find the origin of the notion of democratic sovereignty.[27] Derrida asks us to think about a "democracy to come" which is a democracy without sovereignty. It is a democracy beyond the nation-state sovereignty even beyond citizenship. This leads Derrida to think about a "god without sovereignty."[28] Following this notion of "god without sovereignty" theologians such as John D. Caputo, Merold Westphal and Richard Kearney offered a postmodern de-ontological political theology. John D. Caputo's *The Weakness of God* envisages a week God whose power is the power of powerlessness. For Caputo, God's power is a radical promise, the hope of an event to come, an event absolutely unforeseen and unconditional.[29] The de-ontological political theologies uphold the hope for the radical democracy to be-come the power of the weak and the vulnerable.

Catherine Keller is another postmodern theologian who is committed to thinking of God without sovereignty. Apart from Derrida, she is influenced also by the Whiteheadian process thought, eco-feminism, feminism and Gilles Deleuze. Keller speaks about a God of becoming in contradictory to the traditional Western notion of the Omni-God. By critiquing the unilateral-masculine power of God, Keller proposes a theo-poetics of love. Keller contends that "a constructive theology of becoming sustains a political theology of love."[30] Keller's theology of becoming eschews the notion of sovereignty and envisions a relational ontology. This relational ontology is closely linked with our public life and the planet earth which is clearly explained in her book *Political Theology of the Earth: Our Planetary Emergency and the Struggle for a New Public*. Founding on a broad planetary movement of social and ecological justice, in this book, Keller calls for dissolving the division between religious and the secular.[31]

Towards a Radical Political Theology: About this Book Project

However, the radical political theology takes an unprecedented way of theologizing in the contemporary context of neoliberalism and the global capitalism. Following the post-Western (post-Continental) political philosophies of Slavoj Zizek, Giorgio Agamben, Alain Badiou, Antonio Negri, Jean Luc Nancy and Gilles Deleuze, the radical theologians such as Clayton Crockett, Ward Blanton, Jeffrey Robins, Noelle Vahanian, Karen Bray and Edward Waggoner offer a new turn towards "new materialism." They take the cue from the Marxian, the Nietzschean, and the late-Derridean critique of the monotheist Christianity (Nietzsche calls it "monotonotheism") and thereby envisage a radical politics which is de-linked with the divine sovereignty. In line with Jean-Luc Nancy who deconstructs Christianity from its rigid monotheism and envisages a God of transimmanence, the radical political theologians take about a de-transcendentalized God (Spivak) who is ontologically connected with the materiality of the world—the "being thus of the things" (Agamben). Unlike the confessional and the apologetic theologies that always allude to a transcendent/mystic God who legitimises a sovereign state, God of the radical political theology is the internal potentiality of Life (Deleuze) which is inherently multiple and democratic.[32] Life, here, is organically material and political which in turn becomes the potential of the Multitude (Hardt and Negri) irrupting in the even contemporary context of 'repressed sovereignties.'

Following the thread of the 'de-transcendentalzing' theological imagination, radical political theologians interrogate the postmodern American theologies including the death of God theologies of Mark C. Taylor, Charles E. Winguist, and Carl A. Raschke for being inadequate to address the agonistic politics of the dispossessed and the disenfranchised in the crucial context of neoempire. They argue that those theologies are still functioning in the dogmatic and the confessional framework "that puts both theology and politics in an order." For them, the American postmodern theologies are theoretically insufficient to deconstruct the Western theological compromise on sovereignty. Jeffrey Robbins contends that the process theology still remains as a "speculative thought." For him, it "never went so far to put the established Christian theology into question;" rather it "still operates almost exclusively within a Christian confessional framework."[33] However, radical political theologians signify the theopoetics of Catherine Keller in which she engages more with the Deleuzian 'pure materialism' and the Spivakian "planetarity" rather than the Whiteheadian dialectics between the actual and the virtual.

Radical political theology denies the theological project of radical orthodoxy. For the radical political theologians, radical orthodoxy "desires to effect a restoration of a neotraditional orthodoxy which is a triumphalist Christianity that was broken with the emergence of a nontheological secular sphere at the start of European modernity." Furthermore, they held the view that the radical orthodox legitimizes a medieval vision of Christian empire which eliminates democracy as a viable political form in its critique of liberalism in general. In contradictory to the project of radical orthodoxy, radical political theology offers a theology of de-sovereignized God/enfleshed God/enmattered God that becomes a potential space of the Multitude. Radical political theology offers a theology of new materialism where God is freed from transcendence. It is a radical theology that is liberated from the traditional Christian dogmatics and apologetics. It challenges the apologetic and confessional Christianity that celebrates both the political sovereignty and the divine sovereignty and becomes the imperial ontology within. It envisions a deconstructed Christianity which is contradictory to the dogmatic and fundamentalist

Christianity that supports global capitalism. In this radical political theology of new materialism, God becomes virtual and potential. It is this potential that determines the freedom and justice of the coming community (Agamben). Taking the cue of this radical political theology, this book explores the possibility of signifying Ambedkar as a post-Continental philosopher and theologian from India who replaces the Absolute transcendent Brahman with the notion of karuna (compassion) and dismantles the dichotomy between religion and politics by envisaging Dhamma (ethics).

End Notes

1 John D. Caputo and Catherine Keller, *Crosscurrents*, Winter 2007, 105-118 at 108.

2 Giorgio Agamben, *The Kingdom and Glory: For a Theological Genealogy of Economy and Government* (Stanford: Stanford University Press, 2011), 10.

3 Joerg Rieger and Edward Waggoner, eds., *Religious Experience and New Materialism: Movement Matters* (New York: Palgrave Macmillan, 2016); Clayton Crockett and Jeffrey W. Robbins, *Religion, Politics, and the Earth: The New Materialism* (New York: Palgrave Macmillan, 2012); Ward Blanton, Clayton Crockett, Jeffrey W. Robbins, and Noelle Vahanian, *An Insurrectionist Manifesto: Four New Gospels for a Radical Politics* (New York: Columbia University Press, 2016); Clayton Crockett, *Derrida after the End of Writing: Political Theology and New Materialism* (USA: Fordham University Press, 2018).

4 Alistair Kee, ed., *The Scope of Political Theology* (London: SCM Press, 1978), 2.

5 Jan Assmann, *Authority and Salvation: Political Theology in the Ancient Egypt, Israel, and Egypt* (Munich: Carl Hanser, 2000), p. 15 cited by Hent de Vries and Lawrence E. Sullivan, eds. *Political Theologies: Public Religion in a Post-secular World* (Delhi: Orient Longman, 2006), p. 32.

6 Carl Schmitt, *Political Theology: Four Chapters on the Concept of Sovereignty* (Chicago: University of Chicago Press, 1985), 36.

7 Ibid., 6.

8 Jurgen Moltmann, "European Political Theology," in *The Cambridge Companion to Christian Political Theology*, eds., Craig Hovey and Elizabeth Philips (New York: Cambridge University Press, 2015), 8.

9 Johann Baptist Metz, *Theology of the World* (New York: Herder and Herder, 1969), 10.

10 Ibid., 112.

11 Jurgen Moltmann, "Political Theology in Ecumenical Contexts," in F. Schussler Fiorenza, K. Tanner and M. Welker, eds., *Political Theology: Contemporary*

Challenges and Future Directions (Louisville, CY: Westminster John Knox Press, 2013), 2.

12 Ibid., 2; Jurgen Moltmann, *On Human Dignity: Political Theology and Ethics* (London: SCM Press, 1984), 99.

13 Jurgen Moltmann, *The Crucified God* (New York: Harper and Row, 1974), 328.

14 See Clayton Crocket, *Radical Political Theology: Religion and Politics after Liberalism* (New York: Columbia University Press, 2013), 10.

15 Elizabeth Schussler Fiorenza, Jurgen Moltmann, "Prospects for Political Theology in the Face of Contemporary Challenges," in F. Schussler Fiorenza, K. Tanner and M. Welker, eds., *Political Theology: Contemporary Challenges and Future Directions* (Louisville, CY: Westminster John Knox Press, 2013), 25.

16 John Milbank, *Theology and Social Theory* (Cambridge, MA: Blackwell, 1990), 206-9.

17 John Milbank, Catherine Pickstoke, and Graham Ward, eds., *Radical Orthodoxy* (London & New York: Routledge, 1999), 3; Daniel M. Bell. Jr., 'Post liberalism and Radical Orthodoxy" in *The Cambridge Companion to Christian Political Theology*, eds., Craig Hovey and Elizabeth Philips (New York: Cambridge University Press, 2015), 110-132 at 107.

18 Clayton Crockett, *Radical Political Theology*, 12.

19 Daniel M. Bell, "Post liberalism and Radical Orthodoxy," 130.

20 Graham Ward, *Christ and Culture* (London: John Wiley & Sons, 2008), 19.

21 Clayton Crockett, *Radical Political Theology*, 17.

22 Kwok Pui-lan, "Theology and Social Theory," in *Empire and the Christian Tradition: New Readings of Classical Theologians,* Kwok Pui-lan and Don H. Compier (Minneapolis: Fortress Press, 2007), 18.

23 For detailed discussion see, Y. T. Vinayaraj, *Intercessions: Theology, Liturgy, and Politics* (New Delhi: ISPCK, 2016), 6-7.

24 Emmanuel Levinas, *Totality and Infinity, An Essay on Exteriority*, trans by Alphonso Lingis (Pittsburg: Duquesne University Press, 1969).

25 Jean-Luc Marion, *God without Being* (Chicago: Chicago University Press, 1991).

26 Judith Butler, *Parting Ways, Jewishness and Critique of Zionism* (New York: Columbia University Press, 2012); Mayra Rivera, *The Touch of Transcendence, A Postcolonial Theology of Transcendence of God* (Louisville, London: Westminster John Knox, 2007), 65. For a critical study on Levinas and Marion, see Y. T. Vinayaraj, *Dalit Theology after Continental Philosophy* (New York: Palgrave Macmillan, 2016).

27 Jacques Derrida, *Rogues: Two Essays on Reason*, trans. Pascale-Anne Brault and Michael Naas (Stanford: Stanford University Press, 2005), xii; *The Beast and the Sovereign*, Vol. I, trans. Geoffrey Bennington (Chicago: Chicago University Press, 2009).

28 Ibid., 87; Clayton Crockett offers a detailed discussion on Derridean concept of God without sovereignty in Clayton Crocket, *Derrida after the End of Writing*, 43-57.

29 John D. Caputo, *The Weakness of God: A Theology of the Event* (Bloomington: Indiana University Press, 2008), 85.

30 Catherine Keller, *The Face of the Deep: A Theology of Becoming* (London: Routledge, 2003), xv; *God and Power: Counter-Apocalyptic Journeys* (Minneapolis: Augsburg Fortress Press, 2005), 151.

31 Catherine Keller, *Political Theology of the Earth: Our Planetary Emergency and the Struggle for a New Public* (New York: Columbia University Press, 2018).

32 Clayton Crockett, *Radical Political Theology*, 52.

33 Jeffrey Robbins, "Terror and the Postmodern Condition: Toward a Radical Political Theology," in *Religion and Violence in a Secular World: Toward a New Political Theology*, ed., Clayton Crockett (Charlottesville: University of Virginia Press, 2006), 196.

1

Empire, Multitude, and the Church
Political Theology after Hardt and Negri

Michael Hardt and Antonio Negri are the post-continental philosophers who offer us a paradigm shift in the contemporary empire studies and lead us towards a radical vision of democracy and state. Empire, for them, is not the ancient military system or the medieval kingdom; rather it is a net work of international organizations and capitalist corporations. To Hardt and Negri, empire coincides with the very process of globalization. Empire signifies the life in the age of the neo-capitalist culture and politics. Empire is a system of domination and subordination which colonizes peoples' minds, bodies and their territories. It is the "conglomerates of power that are aimed at controlling all aspects of our lives, from macropolitics to our innermost desires."[1] Exposing the biopolitical mechanism of the empire, Hardt and Negri offer us a philosophy of an anti-imperial subjectivity which is called "Multitude." Multitude signifies a radical 'life in common'—a political project of radical democracy in the age of 'corporate capitalism' (Naomi Klein). Engaging with the political philosophy of Michael Hardt and Antonio Negri, this chapter explores the possibility of constructing a radical political theology of the church as it envisions anti-imperial collectivity and egalitarian identity even in the contemporary context of neoempire.

Hardt and Negri: Sketching the Thought-Worlds

Michael Hardt is an American literary theorist and Left-wing political philosopher. He was born in 1960 in Washington DC. Currently Hardt teaches in the literature program at Duke University and serves as the editor of the *South Atlantic Quarterly*. Hardt did his research under the guidance of Negri that made them co-authors of certain books and co-travelers of a radical vision of 'living in common.' Antonio Negri is the Italian Marxist philosopher, born in Padua in 1933. Negri started his career as a professor of political philosophy in the University of Padua. His political engagement made him familiar with Marxism from an early age. He joined the Italian Socialist Party in 1956 and engaged with Marxist movements in 1960s. Negri taught at the Paris VIII (Vincennes) and the College International *de philosophie* along with Jacques Derrida, Michael Foucault and Gilles Deleuze.

Hardt and Negri are known for their Empire trilogy—*Empire* (2000), *Multitude* (2004), and *Commonwealth* (2009). Their most recent book is *Declaration* (2011). Their writings explore the new forms of dominations in the contemporary world and the significance of the new social movements that resist them. The Empire trilogy investigates the political, economic and social aspects of globalization. While explaining the shift from the modern imperialist nation-state centered ruling system to the post-globalized global net-work of power which they call empire, they, on the other hand, approach globalization as a possibility of new resistances within the empire. In their political philosophy, they signify the counter-social movements like encampments and occupation movements through which they envisage effective resistances that democratize our world more meaningfully and creatively.

1. Hardt and Negri as the Postmodern Left

Negri has an important role in the re-conceptualizations of Italian Marxism. Since 1960s Italian scholars have been searching for a critical Marxism, beyond Leninism within and outside of the communist party structure. They found possibility in the several seasons of struggles by the Italian antagonistic movements. Negri was one of them who signified the grassroot people's movements, environmental activism, anti-neoliberal movements and workers movements. Negri participated in the parallel left-wing political actions that helped the Italian anti-capitalist movements to envisage an era of the postmodern left politics. Negri's notion of *Empire* and his subsequent writings along with Hardt stirred up political philosophy and political anthropology further in favor of the re-imagined Marxism and thus offered a theoretical/philosophical foundation for the contemporary Italian Marxist thought.

It is because of their critical engagement with globalization, they are categorized as postmodern left.[2] Capitalism takes new turns in the era of globalization. The neoliberal strategies of the multi-national corporations and the former capitalist countries have been turned to the market-centered, consumeristic public life which has carried on the civil society to a certain kind of apolitical situation. Thus, Hardt and Negri argue that the traditional Marxism has to be re-conceptualized in terms of these changes in the socio-political, economic and cultural aspects of public life in the context of globalization. For them, the Marxian dialectics in between private property and public property, common and communism, religion and politics are to be re-envisaged and the political metamorphosis that happened due to the process of globalization is to be scrutinized in favor of the common people. In their Empire trilogy, *Empire* focuses on the issues of globalization and *Multitude* discusses some of the solutions that bring the commons into the public discourse.

2. The Common in Communism: Rethinking Marxism

Hardt in his essay entitled "The Common in Communism" argues that the concepts like communism, democracy, and freedom have become insignificant in the contemporary emerging context of the neoliberal political economy and culture. Communism has come to mean the state control of economic and social life and thus it has to be re-thought. In the above mentioned essay, he explains his critique of both the neo-liberal strategies of capitalism and the notion of public property offered by socialism. According to Hardt, the neoliberal strategies try to privatize properties and on the other hand, the socialists want to publicize the properties. Instead, he argues for the concept of 'common in communism.' He declares his project: "we need to explore another possibility: neither the private property of capitalism nor the public property of socialism but the common in communism."[3]

The communist hypothesis has to be revised because of the change in the conditions of the capitalist mode of production. Since the technical composition of labor and the social condition of the production have been changed in the era of globalization, Hardt demands a rethinking of Marxism and Communism today. The immaterial and biopolitical production in terms of production of ideas, information, images, knowledges, code, languages, social relationships, affects are no more private properties today; rather they are shared and thus remain common. These 'commons' should not be privatized as it is done by neoliberal capitalism and should not be publicized by the state as it is proposed by socialism. The privatization of the indigenous knowledges by the corporates through the patent rights is a modern form of exploitation and expropriation of the common. Here the common is made private property of the corporates. Thus, for Hardt, the role of Communism today is not to publicize the property; but to make property common. The common refers to the land, water and air as well as to language, knowledges, ideas, images and affects. When these common are privatized or controlled either by the state or the corporates, the productivity is reduced and destroyed. The task is to initiate free access and circulation of common and that is the significance of Communism today.

Re-reading Marxism, Hardt argues that the production not only creates objects but subjects also. Production in the era of globalization is not just commodities but it creates social relations and forms of life also. The immaterial and the biopolitical context of production are to be recognized and acknowledged. It is our notions of social relations, gender positions, and cultural imaginations necessitate and demand certain kind of productions and thus it is nothing but the production and re-production of our own life forms itself. Hardt explains this: "humans produce and humans are produced." Following Michael Foucault, Hardt argues that in this biopolitical production both objects and subjects are humans. It is here Hardt's hypothesis lies: the process of biopolitical production in the context of globalization can be the possibility of reproducing new beings—new humanity. He further explains: "Capital, in other words, is creating its own gravediggers." Making property into common in the era of globalization is the task of Communism. "What property is to Capitalism and state property to Socialism, the common is to Communism."[4]

3. Love as a Political Concept

Hardt and Negri re-define love as a political concept. For them, the modern concept of love is almost 'exclusively limited to the bourgeois couple and the claustrophobic confines of the nuclear family.' Love has become a strictly private affair in the age of globalization. Hardt contends that we need a more generous and more unrestrained conception of love which has political power of transformation. It is here the personal becomes political and love functions as the constituent power of the multitude. Hardt finds religious traditions valid for the conceptualization of the politics of love. Hardt argues that love as a transformative power is so communitarian in the Judaic-Christian religious traditions. According to those traditions, love creates community. On the contrary, love in the era of globalization, is confined to the very personal realm which is apolitical in content. This type of love is nothing but the 'love of the same'—the love based on the racial, familial, and gender love. Hardt opines that the political philosophy of love is destroyed in this neoliberal project of the 'love for the same.'

Love as a political concept is different from the so called 'love for the other.' 'Love for the other' is the charity oriented, sacrifice centered love which is legitimized by the established religions. It is a program that flows down from the top to the bottom. It is not all political, but charity oriented and obligatory in content. On the other hand, Hardt defines love as a political project. For them, love is a proliferation of differences, not the destruction of differences. The love of the differences is the love for the people—the multitude. It demands not the obligation, but martyrdom. The martyrdom that this political love demands is something revolutionary in content the way in which we care about each other. Martyrdom in this political project of love is not a destructive project as it is seen in the terrorist responses; rather, it is an act of love—a constituent act aimed at the future against the sovereignty of the present. Here love becomes political and poetical since it is waiting for the radical democracy to come. Hardt and Negri explain the project of love explicitly as a political concept:

> We need to recover today this material and political sense of love, a love as strong as death. This does not mean that you cannot love your spouse, your mother, and your child. It only means that your love does not end there, that love serves as the basis for our political projects in common and constitution of a new society. Without this love, we are nothing.[5]

Hardt and Negri trace the theological understanding of the Church in this political manifestation of love and the making of Multitude. Despite the conceptual similarity between Church and Multitude, Hardt and Negri warns us any kind of appropriation between them, since the Church always stand in favour of global capitalism and empire. Love as a political concept that envisages common production and common living, for Hardt and Negri, signifies the failure of the Church to combat global capitalism. At the same time, Multitude as the political project of love offers a potential space for anti-imperial theological imagination. As Jared Woodard rightly said; it would be a hermeneutical violence, if we identify Multitude with Church unless and until the Church does the theology of love as a political project, not as a charity program and does the politics crucifying its notion of the sovereign God.[6]

Of course, Multitude is a confessional point for the Church to re-imagine theology as an anti-imperial project.

Empire, Multitude, and Commonwealth

The Empire trilogy (*Empire*, 2000; *Multitude*, 2004; *Commonwealth*, 2009), authored by Hardt and Negri has deeply influenced the postmodern political philosophy as well as the contemporary political theology. The Marxist, Slavoj Zizek once called *Empire* "*the* Communist Manifesto for our times." *Empire* has unleashed radical imaginations of state, democracy and political subjectivity. Hardt and Negri claim that their attempt in *Empire* is to make Marxism relevant once more to the revolutionary project and enrich the new social movements to counter the onslaught of the strategies of the neoliberal projects and programs. *Multitude,* on the other hand, attempts to answer some of the questions that are raised by the critics and reviewers of the first work *Empire*. In *Commonwealth,* they bring out very clear political philosophy of radical democracy in the age of globalization and the neo-liberal cultural imperialism. This section offers a detailed discussion on the themes Empire, Multitude, and Commonwealth as Hardt and Negri propose in their Empire trilogy.

1. Empire

Hardt and Negri's notion of Empire is not to be confused with the medieval/modern imperialism. It is not a military-imperial regime like the Roman Empire or the British Empire or the American Empire. Hardt and Negri opine that such kind of imperialism is over. Empire is neither a haunting memory of an old imperial legacy nor a futuristic promise. For Hardt and Negri, Empire is a current reality in which we are all caught up. It is a postmodern phenomenon in which our economic, cultural, and social values are formed and nurtured. They explain this: "Empire is materializing before our eyes...along with global market and the global circuits of production has emerged a global order, a new logic of structure and rule—in short a new form of sovereignty."[7] The Empire signifies a post-globalized human condition where we see the free flow of capital, information, and technology. It signifies the uneven development of centre and the periphery countries and the irreversible gap between the rich and the poor. Empire, as Negri and Hardt described it, is an imaginative geography of globalization of world space, where boundless flow of capital, labor and information transcend the older imperialist order and yet at the same time, plant the seeds of destruction and transformation of Empire.[8]

However, Empire has no territorial center of power and does not rely on any territorial boundaries. As Negri explains, Empire "is a decentered and deterritorializing apparatus of rule that progressively incorporates the entire global realm within its open, expanding frontiers."[9] It is spread globally. By managing hybridities, differences, and plural exchanges through modulating networks of power, empire offers an imperial subjectivity for all of us whether we like it or not. The notion of empire is not a metaphor for Hardt and Negri; rather it is a theoretical concept about sovereignty. Sovereignty is no more an imperialist concept. In an era of globalization, it has taken the form of a global rule in which our subjectivities are formed in favour of the neoliberal agendas. Empire is a political ontology of sovereignty in which we all form our subjectivities and social imaginations in favour of the neoliberal economy and culture. Hardt and Negri make it clear in their definition of Empire:

> Our basic hypothesis is that sovereignty has taken a new form, composed of a series of national and supranational organisms united under a single logic of rule. This new global form of sovereignty is what we call Empire.[10]

Empire is a "network power" that includes the dominant nation-states, trans-national institutions, capitalist corporations and other powers in a hierarchical order. In the imperial network of power or global governance, not all powers are equal. It is a contradictory system of inequality and hierarchies. However, all partners in this system maintain the order intact to keep up their position within. It is not a peaceful coexistence of cultures, economies, and politics; rather, it is a coexistence of war. Empire exists by creating the state of war or conflict within and without. Empire is a war-centered mechanism. War in Empire is not necessarily about military action;

rather, it is the biopolitical act of "producing and reproducing" of the subjects.[11] Negri and Hardt claim, therefore, that when "life itself is put on center stage, then war becomes properly ontological."[12] It is this ontological war situation that sanctions the suspension of democracy.

Empire is a political ontology. As a constituting power, Empire has no exteriority. It is an ontology which has no outside. Empire is a condition in which all of us are located within. There is no "outside" or "escape." Both domination and resistances are located within a unified space. Resistance does not exceed the boundary of Empire; it happens within the boundary of the Empire. As Negri rightly points out, terrorism is not to deny Empire but to control Empire. This doesn't mean inertia or the end of resistance. Negri prefers the word "exodus" of the mass immigrations and the need to do away with borders.[13] It is the process of doing away with borders that invokes a new global democracy of Multitude. In order to resist the biopower of the Empire, Negri proposes the theory of Multitude as a radical, anti-imperial, political subjectivity that resists Empire from within.

2. Multitude

According to Hardt and Negri, Multitude is the living alternative that grows within Empire.[14] Empire as a network of international organization and capitalist corporations coincides with the process of globalization. In Negri's perspective, there are two types of globalization: (1) Empire that spreads globally its network of hierarchies and divisions that maintain order through new mechanisms of control and constant conflict and (2) new circuits of cooperation and collaboration that stretch across nations and continents and allow an unlimited number of encounters.[15] It is the latter gives rise to the possibility of living in common and acting together while remaining different. For Negri, Multitude is an open network "in which all differences can be expressed freely and equally, a network that provides the means of encounter so that we can work and live in common. While explaining the concept of Multitude, Artemy Magun calls it "negative imperialization."[16]

For Hardt and Negri, "common" is not homogeneity but alterity and difference. Unlike the concept of "people" which is unitary and identitarian, Multitude is many.[17] According to Hardt and Negri, the notion of people reduces the diversity to a unity and makes the population a single identity: "the people" is one. On the other hand, the Multitude is composed of many "irreducible singularities" of cultures, races, ethnicities, genders, and sexual orientations; different forms of labor, different ways of living, different views of the world and different desires. Multitude is multiplicity. Multitude is many-colored. Unlike the masses, in the Multitude, social differences remain different. Multitude goes beyond the category of class which is unitary in concept and logic. Multitude is a new concept of people that even transcends the category of proletariat. The proletariat or the working class refers to all waged workers, separating them from the poor, unpaid domestic laborers, all the traditional workers who do not receive a wage. Rather, Multitude is an inclusive concept. Multitude is thus composed potentiality of all the diverse agents of social production. Thus, the task for the project of Multitude is to manage to communicate and act in common while remaining internally different. In the democracy of Multitude, the economic, cultural, and the social realms enacted together to envisage an alternative life in common. It encourages for the construction of common knowledge, common power, common production and common subjectivity.

Multitude offers a counter political ontology where the production of subjectivities is de-imperialized. As Negri argues, our struggles determine our subjectivities.[18] Whether it is monarchy or democracy the biopower of the sovereignty is exercised on the human bodies and social bodies. Sovereignty helps the Empire to exploit the masses without excluding them within its power dynamics. Giorgio Agamben calls this "state of exception"—excluded but not included.[19] Multitude offers a radical life of freedom even if we remain within the sovereign power. Thus, Multitude is radical concept of constitutive power (*potentia*) that reconstitutes our subjectivities as political subjectivities. It offers us a materialist understanding of body/flesh which is not fixed; rather becoming and belonging–a constitutive ontology as it is well explained by Merleau-Ponty. Negri invokes this political concept of flesh from Merleau-Ponty:

> The primary matter [or: raw material] of the multitude is the flesh, i.e., that common living substance where the body and the intellect coincide and are indistinguishable. Maurice Merleau-Ponty writes: 'the flesh is not matter, nor mind, nor substance. In order to designate it we need the old and new term element, in the same sense as this term was used to speak of water, air, earth, and fire, i.e., in the sense of general thing–a sort of embodied principle that brings a style of being where there is a fragment of being. The flesh is in this sense an element of being.'[20]

Becoming and belonging to the flesh, for Hardt and Negri, is to belong to the potentiality, the life-force, the relation to being. They make it clear: 'like the flesh, the Multitude is oriented towards the fullness of life.' For them, Multitude is "the power to create social relationships in common."[21] Thus, Multitude is a 'revolutionary monster' which appears messianically through which we transform our flesh into new forms of life—a life in common. It is a political ontology of radical commonness, immanence, and sociality at the level of minds, bodies, labor, art, and technology. Hardt and Negri find the political concept of love as the theoretical ground of living in common. Love in a material and political sense is "the constituent power of the Multitude."[22] In short, Multitude is the possibility to envisage a political democracy of "common" in the age of Empire as we are envisaged today in the multiple forms of local struggles for basic necessities of life: food, water, land, and human rights etc.—the "Commonwealth" of humanity.

3. Commonwealth

In their third book in this series, *Commonwealth*, Negri and Hardt propose a possible constitution for the "life in common." Through the notion of *Commonwealth*, they propose a political project of the Multitude to initiate an ethics of democratic political action within and against Empire. *Commonwealth* articulates the anti-imperial social relations and institutional forms of a possible global democracy. It is a democracy that invites all to share and participate in the common, that is, the air, the water, the fruits of the soil, all nature's bounty—the habitat of humanity. While Empire promotes the 'republic of property' that preserves the property against poor, Commonwealth, on the contrary, promotes the Multitude of the poor where the property becomes common. According to Hardt and Negri, the current capitalist-neoliberal economy destroys the common and strives to transform the common goods such as public industries, public welfare, and natural resources into private properties. For Hardt and Negri, it is nothing but a metamorphosis—"a biopolitical turn of the economy."[23] Hence, they propose a radical democratic political ontology of common.

Working on the theory of Multitude and Commonwealth, Michael Marder calls it "vegetal democracy." For Marder, "vegetal democracy" is the "growing with (and the growing-up) of democracy [that] hinges on fostering the capacity to live the countless voices, and especially with the dispersed multiplicity of non-voices and non-identities, that target us both from within and from without: to fall apart in growing-with."[24] Hardt and Negri explain this vegetal sense of political subjectivity:

> The notion of the common does not position humanity separate from nature, as either its exploiter or its custodian, but focuses rather on the practices of interaction, care, and cohabitation in a common world, promoting the beneficial and limiting the detrimental forms of the common. In the era of globalization, issues of maintenance, production and distribution of the common in both senses and in both ecological and socio-economic frameworks became increasingly central.[25]

Commonwealth opens up the Multitude's process of productivity and creativity that can revolutionize our world and institute a shared common wealth. How do we achieve this? Hardt and Negri offers three platforms through which we demand to the existing governments and the various institutions of global governance: (1) governments must provide everyone with the basic means of life, (2) allowing everyone to become capable of participating in the constitution of society, collective self-rule, and constructive interaction with others, (3) open access to the common against the barriers of private property.[26] At the same time, Hardt and Negri are aware of the impossibility of granting these basic needs of the Multitude by the global governance. They put their trust in the politics of love and joy. They affirm: "the path of joy is constantly to open new possibilities to expand our field of imagination, our abilities to feel and be affected, our capacities of action and passion."[27] It is an invitation to follow an ontological project—the project of love. "Expression of joy is the sign of our power." Hardt and Negri conclude their discussion on Common wealth by explaining the political project of joy and laugh:

> Ours is a laugh of creation and joy, anchored solidly in the present. Our free and equal access to thé common, through which we together produce new and greater forms of the common, our liberation from the subordination, our autonomous control of the circuits of the production of social subjectivity, and in general our construction of common practices through singularities compose the multitude are all limitless cycles of our increasing power and joy. While we are instituting happiness, our laughter is as pure as water.[28]

Hardt and Negri, at the same time, speak about the other side of the project of joy and laugh. Against the Empire, this is going to be the laugh of destruction and revolution. They make it clear in the final statement in the book Commonwealth:

> In the long battles against the institutions that corrupt the common, such as the family, the corporation, and the nation, we will spill no end of tears, but still we laugh. And in the struggles against capitalist exploitation, the rule of property, and the destroyers of the common through public and private control, we will suffer terribly, but still we laugh with joy. They will be buried by laughter.[29]

With *Commonwealth*, Negri and Hardt conclude the *trilogy* begun with *Empire* and continued in *Multitude*, proposing an ethics of freedom for living in our common world and articulating a possible constitution for radical democracy in the context of Empire. It is an invitation to search for a political subjectivity which is ontologically connected to the politics of the Multitude. To fight against Empire is to search for a life in common—the habitat of humanity, the *Commonwealth*. What would be a theological response to the question of Empire? How do the concepts of Multitude and Commonwealth engage with the theological notion of *Ekklesia*—the Church? Does this notion of the life in common imply a radical ecclesiology in the contemporary context of Empire? Since Hardt and Negri relate the concept of Multitude with Church—Augustine's "City of Earth," the above questions are valid and significant.

Empire, Multitude and the Church

'Christianity can hardly be understood apart from Empire.'[30] Joerg Rieger, while analyzing the relationship between Church and Empire, offers two different responses. On one side, he argues that early Christianity was a critique of the Roman Empire which constituted the context of the early Christianity. The Jesus' movement and the apostolic traditions envisaged counter imperial communities that denied the imperial practices of exclusion and marginalization. At the same time, Rieger points out that Christianity after the Constantine era assumed a hierarchical/imperial structure. The early ecumenical councils convened by the emperors signify the involvement of the imperial forces in the formulation Christian doctrines and dogmatics.[31] It is really exciting to read Giorgio Agamben, the Italian philosopher/theologian, when he investigates the context of the emergence of the theology of *oikoumene* (economic trinity) in the patristic period over against the totalitarianism of the Constantine political power.[32] Thus, the relationship between the Empire and Church has always been apprehensive and cryptic. This is true as we go through the historical periods of crusades and the modern mission strategies of the Western church colluded with the European colonialism.

Exposing the trajectory of the conviviality between Church and Empire, Elizabeth Schussler Fiorenza offers a theological treatise on the anti-imperial ecclesiology in her incredible work—*The Power of the Word: Scripture and the Rhetoric of Empire.* In this book, as we have seen in the Negri's theory of Multitude and Commonwealth, Fiorenza speaks about the Church as a political space— "the radical democracy of equals."[33] The radical democracy of Fiorenza is the *ekklesia of wo/men* which offers the language and space for the imagination to develop a public religious discourse, "wherein justice, participation, difference, freedom, equality and solidarity set the ethical conditions."[34] Fiorenza, contra the kyriarchal model of the Empire, defines Church as a radical political space where the logic of domination and subordination is denied and equality and justice for all is affirmed. Fiorenza articulates Christian community—Church as the radical democratic assembly among many, the *cosmopolis* of God's very different peoples.[35] In the same vein of thought, alluding to Paul, Alain Badiou signifies the Pauline theology of Christ-Event as the "counter-community of resistance" to envisage a radical ecclesiology in the emerging context of Empire.[36] Richard Horsley's *Paul and Empire* and *Paul and Politics,* offer a convincing case of defining Church as an anti-imperial imagination.[37] In his *Insurrection of the Crucified,* Theodore W. Jennings, Jr., provides another hermeneutical approach for envisaging Church as an anti-imperial community.[38] This section specially engages with the work of Joerg Rieger and Kwok Pui-lan that offers a radical political ecclesiology by appropriating the political philosophy of Hardt and Negri.

1. 'Ecclesia of the Multitude': Joerg Rieger and Kwok Pui-lan

Engaging with Hardt and Negri who embark multitude as the anti-imperial ideology in the contemporary world of neo-liberal capitalism, Joerg Rieger and Kwok Pui-lan envisage the "Ecclesia of the Multitude," in their well-read book *Occupy Religion: Theology of the Multitude.* According to them, the 'church of the multitude' is 'an anti-imperial imagination which deconstructs its hierarchical ontology and other-centered *diakonia,* envisages a radical democratic community of justice and equality for all.' For them, the task before the church in the context of empire is to be the 'church of the multitude'—the excluded and the marginalized.[39] Here empire is envisaged as the hegemonic logic of neo-liberal capitalism which legitimizes the ideology of exclusion, the politics of refugization, and the economy of destitution. Eleazar S. Fernandez envisages ecclesiology as an advocacy for alternative economy, ecology, and ecumenism in the contemporary context of global capitalism.[40] Setting the whole discussion of redefining church in the context of the recent Occupy movement in USA, Rieger and Pui-lan re-imagine the church that happens in the streets and in the Walmarts where people fight against the exclusive policies of the capitalist economy. It is a radical re-imagination of the space and time that demarcates sacred and profane, liturgy and politics, and God and world. For them, the 'church of the multitude' happens in the secular spaces where people experience the God of immanence.[41]

Instead of the Christendom mentality of the present church that facilitates a hierarchical ordering, the 'church of the multitude' offers a platform of hospitality where no one is excluded on the basis of their caste, class, and gender. It is the place where we do away with our exclusive identities and homogenizing tendencies. It is the place where we deny the notions of clericalism and elitism. The wounded ontology of the church is derived from the crucified body of Jesus Christ. The Christic identity provides church a de-imperialized identity where it embodies the agony of the victims of this world. The very constitutive nature of ekklesia is to become a political community of resistance; not to be an apolitical, insensitive and closed community. As Elizabeth Schussler Fiorenza contends, the non-conformist and radical nature of the church is its constitutive memory. Unlike the postmodern theologians like John Milbank and Graham Ward who define church as the graced community of chosen, Pui-lan and Rieger imagine the grace of God as the right of all excluded and ostracized; rather than the privilege of a few.

Church of the multitude believes in the theology of the priesthood of all humanity; because, "all human beings knowingly or not, minister as priest to one another."[42] Liturgy, as it is originally meant, is a public service which is very political in content and practice was manipulated by the established church latter to facilitate its "patriarchal love." Church of the multitude, on the other hand, is constituted for the public service and that is the legitimate point of its call and commission. Instead of chanting the age old hymns and reiterating the liturgies of power, it emerges with new liturgies which are nothing but the agonies of the struggling people and their hopes of survival. Alluding to Marcella Althaus-Reid, Rieger and Pui-lan explain the liturgical theology of the multitude: "sacraments are more than the enclosed encounters with God; rather they act as ways of understanding love, or even ways of having voices of protest symbolically heard."[43] At the same time, church of the multitude is not a passive recipient of the sacraments; rather they are nurtured by a 'habitus of resistance' which will make them productive agents to carry out God's mission in this world.

2. Church as New Humanity: M. M. Thomas

Among the Indian Christian theologians, it was M. M. Thomas who proposed an authentic political ecclesiology in Indian context. Responding to the state of emergency declared at the midnight of June 25-26, 1975, Thomas said: It is nothing but the onslaught on democracy and a betrayal of the nation." Thomas contended that the effort to quell people's revolts for the sake of internal peace, economic progress and self-reliance through a state of emergency was nothing but the repudiation of all human rights envisaged by a welfare state and its democracy. Thomas envisages a participatory democracy where the sovereign power of the state is nullified and the rights of the marginalized are celebrated. Redefining Church as the sign of the secular Koinonia and New Humanity, Thomas envisions Multitude as it destabilizes the logic of Empire.[44] It is here we see a theoretical conviviality between Negri and Thomas.

Thomas' theology of state and democracy is founded on his theology of the Cross. According to Thomas, Jesus's cross is a protest against the sovereignty of the Roman Empire and the act of crucifixion was to nullify its logic of domination and marginalization. Replacing a political victim on the cross, Jesus exemplified his political solidarity and identification. Jesus's cross signifies the end of the totalitarian power and the beginning of a new community—kingdom community—a universal community where there is no dichotomies. In the new community, "there is no longer any distinction between gentiles and Jews, circumcised and uncircumcised, barbarians, savages, slaves and free; but Christ is all and in all" (Col. 3:11). The new human community is constituted as a single body—the body of the crucified God in history. The crucified body of Christ is not a new thing; rather it is the body of the slain lamb from the creation of the world and it continues to be slain till the end of the world fighting against the totalitarian forces of powers. The mark of crucifixion continues to be the sign of the suffering struggle of God against the principalities and powers till the end of the world. The mission of the Church today is to embody this mark of crucifixion and to reconstitute its ontology in solidarity with the victims of the world.

According to Thomas, the Church is entrusted with a prophetic *diakonia* to discharge its duty based on the servant-hood exemplified by the crucified God. Thomas writes: "The church in India is called to proclaim the gospel of the crucified and risen Christ as the source of redemption of all spiritualties underlying religion as well as ideologies, and to demonstrate the Koinonia in Christ around the Eucharist as the nucleus of a movement of the larger Koinonia in Christ uniting peoples of diverse religions, ideologies and cultures—as well as the cosmos with its bio-diversity."[45] Based on his theology of cross, M. M. Thomas explains the features of the mission of the church in India: (1) the calling of the church is to resist the idolatry of power and wealth and other gods of death in India's collective life, (2) to be in solidarity with the poor and the oppressed in their struggle for justice, and (3) to give up communal self-interest and self-identity for the sake of creating in India a secular national community in the midst of India's religious and ideological pluralism through manifesting a fellowship in Christ, transcending class, caste, ethnic and religious communal divisions.[46]

Thomas's theology of humanization through which he upholds as the hope of the future of humanity makes him so significant among the contemporary political theoreticians of Multitude. Thomas finds the foundation for his eschatological anthropology in the theology of Spirit who raised Jesus from the dead, as the first fruits of the New Creation. Thomas's hope in the future of humanity is incorporated in his understanding of the Risen Christ and His coming. He cites Paul: "We await a Saviour, the Lord Jesus Christ who will change our lowly body to be like his glorious body, by the power which enables him even to subject all to himself" (Phil.3:20-21). Becoming the tortured body of Christ, the Church is being composed and constituted as a Multitude to resist the logic of Empire theologically, liturgically, and hermeneutically. According to Thomas, it is this call and the composition of the Church to be and becoming Multitude only signifies its relevance in the contemporary context of Empire.

Conclusion

The political philosophy of Hardt and Negri is significant in India today as we encounter neoempire in various realms of culture, politics and economy. Empire as the capitalist economy and culture legitimizes corporatism in favour of the elites and the privileged and accentuates impoverishment and destitution. The recent crisis in the issue of migrant labors and the suicide of the farmers are the real evidences of this neo-capitalist economy and culture. Welfare-state, social democracy and the rights endowed citizens have become insignificant words and they have nothing to do with our current public policy and projects. The judiciary and the legislature are either controlled or manipulated in favour of the corporate elites. The nexus between corporate forces and Hindutva ideologues legitimizes a multifaceted sovereign political power which formulates a hegemonic biopolitics of hatred and violence. Violence against dalits, women, religious minorities, sexual minorities, and migrant labours are rampant. On the other hand, the national elites, the multinational corporations, the international nuclear regimes, find home in India. In this crucial context of deprivation and vulnerability, theology of the multitude becomes decisive for the Church in India. The radical ecclesiology challenges the Church in India to realize its call to become a political ontology of the Multitude in the context of neoempire. Radical ecclesiology is a call within the call of the Church to become a "weak church" of the Crucified Christ by becoming the body of the crucified people "now." The contemporary people movements for the preservation of life resources: land, water and forest, the resistances of the dalits and women for the right to life and dignity, the political insurgence of refugees and migrant labours etc., appear before the Church in India not as its diaconal spaces but as the kenotic spaces through which the Church finds its "weak ontology" as the church of the Multitude.

End Notes

1 Jeorg Rieger, *Christ and Empire: From Paul to Postcolonial Times* (Minneapolis: Fortress Press, 2007), vii.
2 Nicholas Tampio, "Assemblages and the Multitude: Deleuze, Hardt, Negri, and the Postmodern Left," in *European Journal Of Political Theory* 2009: 8; 383-400.
3 Michael Hardt, *The Common in Communism, Re-thinking Marxism: A Journal of Economics, Culture and Society*, 22:3, 346-356 (July 2010).
4 Ibid., 348.
5 Hardt and Negri cited by Leonard Schwartz, *A Conversation with Michael Hardt on the Politics of Love, Interval(le)s II.2-III-1* (Fall 2008/ winter 2009).
6 Jared Woodard, "Waiting for the Multitude," *Journal for Cultural and Religious Theory*, vol. 6 no. 1 (December 2004), 122-132.
7 Antonio Negri & Michael Hardt, *Empire* (Cambridge, MA, and London: Harvard University Press, 2000).
8 Ibid., 137.
9 Antonio Negri & Michael Hardt, *Multitude: War and Democracy in the Age of Empire* (New York: Penguin Press, 2004), xiii.
10 Antonio Negri & Michael Hardt, *Empire*, xii.
11 Antonio Negri & Michael Hardt, *Multitude*, 13.
12 Ibid., 19.
13 Ibid., 156.
14 Ibid., xiii.
15 Ibid., xiii.
16 Artemy Magun, Negative Imperialization," in *Politics of the One: Concepts of the One and the Many in Contemporary Thought*, edited by Artemy Magun (New York & London: Bloomsbury, 2013), 127-201.
17 Antonio Negri & Michael Hardt, *Multitude*, xvii.
18 Ibid., 197.
19 Giorgio Agamben, *State of Exception* (Chicago: The University of Chicago Press, 2005).
20 Antonio Negri & Michael Hardt, *Commonwealth* (Cambridge, MA: Harvard University Press, 2009), 30.
21 Antonio Negri & Michael Hardt, *Multitude*, 329.
22 Ibid., 352.
23 Ibid., 152.

24 Michael Marder, "Vegetal Democracy: The Plant that is not One" in *Politics of the One: Concepts of the One and Many in Contemporary Thought,* ed. Artemy Magun (New York: Bloomsbury, 2013), 128.
25 Antonio Negri & Michael Hardt, *Commonwealth,* viii.
26 Ibid., 381.
27 Ibid., 379.
28 Ibid., 383.
29 Ibid., 383.
30 Joerg Rieger," Christian Theology and Empires," in *Empire and Christian Traditions: New Readings of Classical Theologians,* eds. Kwok Pui-lan and Compier Don H (Minneapolis: Fordham Press, 2007), 1.
31 Ibid., 9.
32 Giorgio Agamben, *The Kingdom and Glory: For a Theological Genealogy of Economy and Government* (Stanford: Stanford University Press, 2011), 50-51.
33 Elizabeth Schussler Fiorenza, *The Power of the Word: Scripture and the Rhetoric of Empire* (Minneapolis: Fortress Press, 2007).
34 Adriana Hernandez, *Pedagogy, Democracy, and Feminism: Rethinking the Public Sphere* (New York: State University of New York Press, 1997), 31.
35 Elizabeth Schussler Fiorenza, *The Power of the Word: Scripture and the Rhetoric of Empire.*
36 Alain Badiou, *Saint Paul: The Foundation of Universalism,* trans. Ray Brassier (Stanford: Stanford University Press, 2003).
37 Richard Horsley, ed., *Paul and Empire: Religion and Power in Roman Imperial Society* (Harrisburg, P.A: Trinity Press, 1997).
38 Theodore W. Jennings Jr., *The Insurrection of the Crucified: The "Gospel of Mark" as Theological Manifesto* (Chicago, IL: exploration Press, 2003).
39 Joerg Rieger and Kwok Pui-lan, *Occupy Religion: Theology of the Multitude* (New York & UK: Rowman & Littlefield Publishers, 2012), 99.
40 Eleazar S. Fernandez, "The Church as a Household of Life Abundant: Reimagining the Church in the Context of Global Economics," in *Theology that Matters: Ecology, Economy and God,* ed. Darby Kathleen Ray (Minneapolis: Fortress Press, 2006), 172 & 177.
41 Ibid., 102.
42 Ibid., 115.
43 Ibid., 117.
44 Y. T. Vinayaraj, "Empire, Multitude, and the Church: Signifying M. M. Thomas for a Theology of Multitude in India," in *Reclaiming Manyness: Re-reading M. M. Thomas in the Light of Indian Christian Theologies,* edited by P. G. George and Y. T. Vinayaraj (Kolkata: SATHRI, 2015), 119.
45 M. M. Thomas, *A Diaconal Approach to Indian Ecclesiology* (Rome & Tiruvalla: CIIS & CSS, 1995), 82.
46 M. M. Thomas, "The Church in India—Witness to the Meaning of the Cross Today," in *Future of the Church in India,* ed. Aruna Gnanadason (Nagpur: NCCI, 1990), 11.

2

Subalternity, Marginality, and Planetarity
Spivak and the Postcolonial Political Theology

Gayatri Chakravorty Spivak is a well acclaimed literary critic whose works signaled a postcolonial shift in the continental political thought. The core of the Spivakian postcolonial political thought is that she attends to the process of the 'worlding' or the 'othering' of the (gendered) subaltern—the most excluded and marginalized women—by the colonial, western, dominant institutional and cultural discourses. The whole intention of this political project is to redeem the 'irreducible singularity' of the (gendered) subaltern who have been silenced and muted in and through the dominant-colonial representations. This focus has evoked the process of re-reading and re-inscribing the subaltern historiographies and has problematized notions of power, resistance, knowledge and memory implied in the process of 'othering' of the subaltern. Spivakian method of 'de-othering' the subaltern demands the contemporary literary/cultural studies and theological programs to seek new ways of representing or re-presencing the subaltern/the marginalized. This chapter engages with the Spivakian political thought in order to construct a

Postcolonial political theology so as to reclaim the social agency and the political potential of the subaltern in the contemporary context of neoempire.

Spivak: Biography and Epistemology

Positioning Spivak is a risky job. Both her biography and epistemology position her in a state of 'in-between.' Her biographical 'in-betweenness' is well-explained in this statement: "I have a mother and that's Calcutta, and I have a nurturing stepmother and that's the United States. Both are ugly. I feel I have earned the right to critique both two places."[1] Of course, the 'in-between' space, for Spivak, is a critical/interactive/interrogative space that re-defines her ontology, epistemology and politics. She comments about her epistemological position: "My position is generally a reactive one. I am viewed by Marxists as too codic, by feminists as too-male identified, by indigenous theorists as too committed to Western Theory. I am uneasily pleased about this."[2] For Spivak, whether it is biological or epistemological, the 'in-between' space is a 'postcolonial space' in which the dichotomy between east and west, subaltern and elite, centre and margin, religion and politics, secular and sacred, theory and practice is destabilized and deconstructed. It is here the Spivakian epistemology becomes political proclamation of self-reflexivity in the postcolonial context. This section tries to trace her biographical trajectories and the epistemological itineraries by which she invokes us to feel the liminality of her life of 'in-between.'

1. Spivak: Life and Works

Spivak was born into a Bengali middle class Hindu-Brahman family on 24th February 1942, five years before the independence. She thus claims that she "belonged to the first generation of Indian intellectuals after independence."[3] Unlike the other children of the same origin, she went to a mission school led by Adivasi/Tribal Christian converts. Miriam Nandi opines that Spivak's primary education in the Adivasi school might have made her sensitive to the social realities and responsibilities.[4] In 1959 she received an undergraduate degree in English from the University of Calcutta.

She borrowed money to go to the US in the early 1960s to do graduate work at the University of Cornwell. She pursued her PhD there while teaching at the University of Iowa. Spivak's PhD dissertation was on W. B. Yeats (published as *Myself Must I Remake: The Life and Poetry of W. B. Yeats*, 1974) guided by Paul de Man—a born deconstructionist. It was Paul de Man who let her go deep into the Derridean discourses on 'Deconstruction.' Latter on Derrida became an influential philosopher for her whom she describes as 'the important philosopher of the 20th century.'[5] Spivak translated Derrida's work 'De grammatologie' in 1967 and wrote the preface which was described as "setting a new standard for self-reflexivity in prefaces."[6] In 1960, she was briefly married to Talbot Spivak, an American whose name she kept.

Today Spivak has earned international reputation as a literary critic and an eminent teacher. She has taught and given lectures in various universities in the world including UT-Austin/Texas, Universite P. Valery/Montpelier-France, Jawaharlal Nehru University/New Delhi-India, Stanford/California, University of British Columbia/Canada, Goethe-University/Frankfurt-Germany, Riyadh University/Saudi Arabia, and the University of Science and Technology/Hong Kong. Currently she holds the Avalon Foundation Professor of the Humanities at the Columbia University of New York. Spivak has involved in different social-activist programmes in India and US. In 1997, she founded a non-profit organization that provides quality education for children in rural areas of West Bengal. She also trains the local teachers to listen and respond to the educational aspirations of the rural children in India.

Spivak's publications include translations, books and numerous articles. The first and famous of her translation is Derrida's *Of Grammatology* (Johns Hopkins University Press, 1976). Her major publications include *In Other Worlds: Essays in Cultural Politics* (Routledge, 1987); "Can the Subaltern Speak?" in Cary Nelson and Larry Grossberg, eds. *Marxism and the Interpretation of Culture* (Chicago: University of Illinois Press, 1988); *Selected Subaltern Studies*, ed. Ranajit Guha (Oxford: Oxford UP, 1988), *The Post-Colonial Critic: Interviews, Strategies, Dialogues,* ed. Sarah Harasym (London: Routledge, 1990), *Outside in the Teaching Machine*

(Routledge, 1993); *Thinking Academic Freedom in Gendered Post-Coloniality* (University of Cape Town Press, 1993); *A Critique of Postcolonial Reason: Toward a History of the Vanishing Present* (Harvard University Press, 1999); *Death of a Discipline* (Columbia University Press, 2003); *Other Asias* (Blackwell, 2007), and *An Aesthetic Education in The Era of Globalization* (London: Harvard University Press, 2012).

Spivak often describes her literary methodology as 'itinerary'—a journey back and forth between thinking, research, writing and teaching.[7] Spivakian approach is so complex, as she intersects and interrogates various theories, disciplines and methods in her thinking and writing. Kwok Pui-lan calls it 'dancing methodology.'[8] Spivak uses Marxism, Feminism, postmodernism, poststructuralism, postcolonialism, etc., and allow them to interact with and interrogate each other. Stephen Morton provides a rationale for this intentional 'trans-disciplinarity' of Spivakian method. According to Morton, the purpose of the disruption of various disciplines in Spivakian methodology is for "rendering the voices, histories and experiences of the disempowered and the disenfranchised intelligible to her readers."[9] Many writers have termed her approach 'postcolonial deconstruction,' which is unique in both postcolonial and postmodern traditions.

2. Spivak as a 'Postcolonialist'

Spivakian postcolonialism takes a new turn from the conventional postcolonial theory. Departing from the question of the representation of the 'Third World' as it was proposed by Edward Said's *Orientalism,* Spivak questions the essentialist location of the other and exposed its complexity and heterogeneity. Said had argued that 'Orientalism is nothing but a political program of the construction of the other. For him, 'the Orient' is reconstructed, reassembled, and crafted in short, born out of the Orientalists' efforts.'[10] However, unlike Said, who uses a totalizing vision to see the strategy of colonialism and discursive hegemony in perspective, Spivak attempts for a 'postcolonial deconstruction' through which she prefers a 'persistent critique' of the logic of western rhetoric in representing its other. Sumit Chakrabarti clearly distinguishes between Said and Spivak and opines that 'unlike Said who evaluates the architecture of the discursive socio-political apparatus based on the Foucauldian theory of knowledge and power, Spivak sneaks into dead ends to subvert the logic of the dominant western rhetoric as it was informed by Derridean deconstruction.'[11] Spivak does not follow a totalizing vision of an imperialist culture; rather, she prefers a disruptive, interventional, and fragmentary method which differentiates her from typical postcolonialists. Thus, even though she has been designated one among the 'postcolonial trinity,' Spivak locates herself in a contestatory position within postcolonial academia.[12]

3. Spivak as a 'Deconstructionist'

Spivak uses Derridean deconstruction as a starting point of her writing. She considers deconstruction as "a corrective and a critical movement that teaches us to look at limits and questions."[13] According to Spivak, deconstruction is "a persistent critique of what one cannot want."[14] By using deconstruction as a 'radical interruption,' Spivak offers an interventionist approach which begins with the question of the representation of the (gendered) subaltern by the *Subaltern Studies Collective* in India. Her interventionist approach begins from the Third World representations of the (gendered) subaltern and extends to the western discourses, clearly explicating her complex method of postcolonial deconstructive feminism.[15] Sumit Chakrabarti argues that Spivak's strategic use of deconstruction is an affirmative deconstruction through which she enables "a constant effect of engendering of the social positioning and its ever-present heterogeneity within a class or a group or a collective consciousness."[16] This affirmative deconstruction helps Spivak to overcome the Derridean failure to attend to the 'concrete other.' Unlike Derrida, the otherness of the other is not an absolute otherness in Spivak, rather, it is an 'irreducible other' and even 'quite-other.' According to Mayra Rivera, Spivakian deconstruction envisages an experience of 'relational transcendence' where the self-other dyad is disrupted and re-imagined for new incarnations.[17]

4. Spivak as a 'Post-Marxist'

By re-reading Marx through the lens of Derrida, Spivak illumines the Marxian dichotomy between *Vertreten* (proxy) and *darstellen* (portrait) in order to expose the politics and dilemmas inherent in representation.[18] Spivak rejects both the idea that "the masses" are known to themselves and able to make their interests manifest politically (Foucault and Deleuze), and the idea that intellectuals can fulfill their political responsibility by representing or speaking for the masses (Marx).[19] Spivak's criticism of the *Subaltern Studies Collective,* who draws heavily on the Foucault-Deleuze conversation, is that by constituting a self-speaking postcolonial subject as an 'essentialist other', and trying to speak for them in effect, the 'true subaltern' becomes silent. Spivak critiques the Deleuzian usage of 'workers struggle,' that which neglects the "textures of power" in the context of colonialism. Spivak's problem with the poststructural philosophers is based mainly on their ignorance of the positional relations of the dominant to the subaltern.

Spivak interrogates western intellectuals for taking their privileged subjectivity for granted while trying to expose their disregard for the questions of ethnicity, race, and empire in the context of globalization. She stresses the imperative of a self-reflexive position in the context of theory: "What we are asking for is that… the holders of hegemonic discourse should de-hegemonize their position and themselves learn how to occupy the subject position."[20] The intention behind this de-hegemonizing theory is to affirm the *radical alterity* of the subaltern and on the other hand, to destabilize the 'radical autonomy'-the claim of the authenticity of the "real experience" of the (gendered) subaltern.

5. Spivak as a 'Post-Feminist'

Even though Spivak uses the western feminist thought in her writings, she is critical of its universal and generalized approach. While attending to euro-centric feminism, Spivak problematizes the colonial (mis)-representation of the experiences of gendered subaltern in the 'Third World' and its inadequacy to proxy any other particular experiences like the subaltern women in the South. Spivak criticizes the French *avant garde* Feminism that homogenizes the experiences of women irrespective of their cultural and geographical differences. She writes:

> This is a set of directives for class-and race privileged literary women who can ignore the seductive effects of identifying with the values of the other side while rejecting their validity; and, by identifying the political with the temporal and linguistic, ignore as well the micrology of political economy.[21]

Spivak exhorts the French feminists like Kristeva and Irigaray to 'learn to stop feeling privileged as woman.'[22] For Spivak, International Feminism is nothing but a discourse of the North. She criticizes that these are the universal liberation discourses of the metropolitan, 'emancipated,' white middle-class women who want others to become like themselves.[23] Critically engaging with Julia Kristeva's novel 'About Chinese Women' (1977) and Charlotte Bronte's novel *Jane Eyre* (1847), Spivak exemplifies her theory of cauterization of the subaltern by representing them in the Eurocentric textualities. Through these textualities, the Third World women are stereotyped and given fixed subjectivities of victimization. She contends that this "matronizing and sororizing of women in developed countries is also a way of silencing to the subaltern."[24] Critiquing the benevolent global ethics of the international economic agencies who homogenize women labor and the value of production and mis-represent them in an 'othered space,' Spivak signifies her argument that the involvement of the First World intellectuals in Third World academy functions self-interestedly as a process of self-constitution and in turn, the other constitution.[25] On the other hand, Spivak points towards the emergence of the 'new subaltern' and proposes a theory of *planetarity* that takes us from the discourses of the ethics of human rights and love for the other to a de-othered globality through which the *other* is revisited and the self is re-imagined in a globalized era.

6. Spivakian Methodology in a Nutshell

Whether it is Postcolonialism or Poststructuralism or Feminism or Marxism, Spivak seems to be skeptical of any kind of totalizing ideologies and meta-theories as they are 'deeply marked' by colonial imprints. For this reason, she strategically uses the concept *postcoloniality* as a rhetorical space where the colonial epistemological violence is encountered and the subaltern subjectivity is re-imagined as a non-essential category. It is this rhetorical space of postcoloniality which makes Spivakian approach different from other postcolonialists like Homi Bhabha and Ashis Nandy. Spivakian approach denies any kind of essentialist position such as elitism and subalternity. On the other hand, Spivakian subalternity is a de-othered social location. As Ritu Birla clearly explains, it is a call to "quite-other," or an invocation to the social location of alterity, that is, that which escapes consolidation into narrative and identity.[26] Sangeeta Ray's comment on Spivakian methodology is quite meaningful and self-explanatory:

> Spivakian methodology hinges on the following: acknowledging complicity, learning to learn from below, unlearning one's privilege as loss, working without guarantees, persistently critiquing the structures that one inhabits intimately and that one cannot say no to, and giving attention to subject formation such that it "produces the reflexive basis for self-conscious social agency.[27]

In short, postcolonial deconstructionist feminist epistemology seems to be the methodological focal point of Spivak through which she tries to attend to the issues of the colonized, disempowered, marginalized, and disenfranchised other—the (gendered) subaltern in the Third World. Spivakian theory of subaltern embarks on a 'postcolonial turn' in the contemporary global culture, politics, philosophy and theology which makes her an indispensable interlocutor for a contemporary political theology.

The Spectrality of the Spivakian Political Thought

Spivakian theoretical framework is explained in this section by focusing on her three concepts, *subalternity*, *marginality*, and *planetarity* through which she tries to challenge the colonial institutional violence embodied in the 'othering' of the (gendered subaltern) in the South. Spivak uses the above categories as interchangeable and interconnected in order to expose the 'irreducible singularity' of the (gendered) subaltern. It is a 'postcolonial space' in which the subaltern even de-stabilizes its subalternity in the social hierarchy and assumes a de-othered identity or alterity. This alterity is connected with a radical subjectivity of planetarity. Unlike the other continental philosophers, Spivakian political thought offers a contemporary political theory of radical subjectivity for subalterns which makes her the philosopher of subalternity.

1. Subalternity

Defining *subalternity* seems to be Spivak's basic theoretical issue. The use of the term *subaltern* is primarily informed by the work of the Italian Marxist thinker Antonio Gramsci on the rural-based Italian *peasantry* and the research of the international *Subaltern Studies Collective*[28] on the histories of subaltern insurgency in colonial and postcolonial South Asia. In the program of the *Subaltern Studies Collective*, this Gramscian category was used to signify the unprivileged social classes and groups who were denied access to the social and political practices in India.[29] The *Subaltern Studies Collective* sought to re-read and re-write the established historiography of Indian nationalism that had been dominated by elitism and bourgeoisiesm as a consequence of British colonialism.[30] By critiquing the *Collective* to give voice to the voiceless subaltern in India, Spivak asserts that "there is no unrepresentable subaltern subject that can know and speak itself" and asks, "With what voice-consciousness can the subaltern speak?"[31]

The Spivakian thesis is double bind; on one hand, she argues that the colonialists and postcolonials have (mis-)represented the subaltern subject in the colonial-elitist textualities and on the other hand, there cannot be an 'essentialist subaltern subject' to speak against colonial/postcolonial (native) representation as it was proposed by the *Subaltern Studies Collective.* It is out of this epistemological context that the Spivakian thesis arises: "The *subaltern* cannot speak themselves."[32] For Spivak, the voice of the subaltern cannot be heard because its language cannot be understood within the dominant discourse. Spivak explains this: "The subaltern cannot speak means: even when the subaltern makes an effort to the death to speak, she is not able to be heard, and speaking and hearing complete the speech act."[33] The subaltern speech is nothing but the re-presented speech through which the elites speak for the subaltern. Thus, in effect, the real voice of the subaltern is cauterized. Spivak addresses this phenomenon as the unspeakability of the subaltern.

The question of the 'unspeakability' of *subalternity* is further extended to the question of gender. By focusing on women as *subaltern,* Spivak asserts that "within this effaced itinerary of the subaltern, the track of sexual difference is doubly effaced."[34] Spivak explains this doubly effaced female subjectivity by entering into the discussion of the psychobiography of *Sati* (widow-immolation) in pre-colonial India. According to Spivak, women as *subaltern* have had their voices silenced in between the 'imperialist/colonialist object-constitution and the patriarchal subject-formation. She argues that the voices of the sexed subaltern subjectivity has been lost in between the notion of the 'liberative act' of the imperialists who tried to abolish this 'crime' in the name of civilization and the patriarchal notion of *Sati* as a "heroic act" through which it was translated as the subaltern women "wanted to die." For Spivak, the voice of the female subaltern subjectivity is silenced in between the colonial and patriarchal translations of their consciousnesses.

Spivak explicates her thesis—"Can the subaltern Speak?" through a very specific story-the story of Bhubaneswari Bhaduri-a young woman of sixteen or seventeen who hanged herself in her father's house in Calcutta in 1926. It was alleged that she had entered into an illegitimate relationship. However, she was menstruating at the time, which would indicate that she was not pregnant. Years later it emerged that she had killed herself because she had been unable to carry out a mission for a revolutionary group of which she was a member. According to Spivak, Bhubaneswari's suicide was an act of *subaltern* re-writing of the social text of *Sati*-suicide. Yet the "message" self-inscribed on her body was not read. "She 'spoke' but the women did not, do not, 'hear her."

Spivak problematizes the audibility of subaltern voices. According to Spivak, the non-audibility of the subaltern women is not a failure of articulation but the result of the failure of representation.[35] The subaltern speaks but it cannot be heard. Spivak argues that while the intellectuals claim that the subaltern can speak for themselves, they assume the position of 'proxy' and the voice of the 'true' subaltern remains as *aporia.*[36] It is out of this theoretical lacuna of representation that Spivak proposes what she calls the 'strategic use of positive essentialism in a scrupulously visible political interest'. For Spivak, it is a political space of alterity and difference which has nothing to do with *identitarianism*. Spivakian theory of subalternity doesn't support any kind of essentialism and Identitarianism.

Spivakian notion of *subalternity* is a political position-a 'decolonized space'- which means 'without a place in the colonial scheme.'[37] She denies that it is a synonym for the word 'oppressed' or any identitarian positionality. Spivak explains: "if the subaltern speaks, and it is heard; then he or she is not a subaltern."[38] For Spivak, subalternity is a 'rhetorical space' that cuts across any essentialist position in terms of caste, class, gender and geography. If the subaltern speaks, it is an 'Echo,'[39] a 'secret' which is impossible for any kind of gazing, cognition, or representation without deconstruction. What is most dynamic in the assumption of *Spivakian subalternity* is that it destabilizes the 'epistemic violence' of the 'othering' of the subaltern, and it postpones the 'truth' of *subalternity* in order to rescue it from any kind of representation or 'worlding' in history, culture, politics and theology.

2. Marginality

Spivakian notion of *marginality* is an extended idea of her theory of *subalternity*. As in the case of *subalternity*, *marginality* signifies the 'rhetorical space' that denies its obligation to the center. Spivak talks about a different kind of *marginality*, which denies the marginality of the margin and the centrality of the center. In the Spivakian understanding of *marginality*, the notion of center crumbles and thus the margin becomes a non-margin. Spivak theorizes a non-essentialist, heterogeneous and contestatory location of *marginality* that erupts at the center. *Marginality*, just like *subalternity*, is an *aporetic* space of impossibility which cannot be simply represented or assimilated. She probes the notions of *margin* and *marginality* while theorizing her own location as an intellectual from the 'Third World' in a 'First World academy:

> A word to name the margin. Perhaps that is what the audience wanted to hear: a voice from the margin. If there is a buzzword in cultural critique now; it is 'marginality.' Every academic knows that one cannot do without labels. To this particular label, however, Foucault's caution must be applied and we must attend to its *Herkunft* or descent. When a cultural identity is thrust upon one because the center wants an identifiable margin claims for marginality assure validation from the center.[40]

For Spivak, *marginality* is an assumed location where the problem of 'worlding' of the other is re-positioned. It is a theoretical position to challenge the privileged position of Eurocentric/elitist knowledges. Thus, it is a location of *postcoloniality*. While theorizing the transfiguration of the 'Native Informant' to the 'New Immigrant' in the financialized global economy, Spivak de-ontologizes the *subaltern* as it points towards her own location 'in other worlds.'[41] According to Spivak, in the period of Bretton Woods agencies and the World Trade Organization, which represent the indigenous subaltern as the source of trade related intellectual property, the logic of the inaccessibility of marginality to the center is to be rethought. She says that the indigenous subaltern is now turning to a 'new global subaltern' in the logic of global capital.[42] The indigenous cultural traditions are becoming the focus of the capitalist global media. Subalternity has to be repositioned in the new globality. In sum, marginality is not a fixed location that demands the validation from the center; rather, it is a deconstructive space that upholds its 'irreducible singularity' and alterity, which signals the ethical re-positioning of oneself in relation to the 'other.'

Both Spivakian subalternity and marginality problematize the representation of the other and re-imagines it in terms of alterity and irreducible difference. When the privileged people speak for the other, it in fact further cauterizes the other. She relentlessly questions the ability of the 'self' to empty itself to represent the other. It may seem that she is advocating quietism. On the other hand, alluding to Derridean deconstruction, she challenges us to keep on trying to learn to learn from below. To learn from the below is easy. But, how to learn to learn from the below keeps us always in a process of impossible possibility. It is to listen to the 'Echo'—the silenced memory of the marginalized other. It is not an easy job. It is a deconstructive politics similar to catching the lightning and then bottling it. Stephen Morton rightly characterizes it: "Against silencing and foreclosure of the subaltern, Spivak's deconstructive reflections on responsibility and ethical dialogue work towards imagining the conditions of possibility for an ethical dialogue to take place."[43]

For Spivak, even though the marginalized other is a concrete other, it is impossible to enter into its space. It is easy to locate a marginalized other or a subaltern, but it is impossible to learn the other without keeping the self-ego intact. In other words, it is difficult to learn to unravel the hegemonic system that constructs both the other and the self. As Simmons comments, it is a self-suspending leap into the other's sea.[44] Alluding again to Derrida, Spivak contends that learning to learn from below requires *teleopoiesis*. For Derrida, *teleopoiesis* becomes the process of creating toward an ever-distant future (*a-venir*). By adding the question of space, contrary to Derrida, Spivak defines it as the process of creating toward a distant future with a "distant other." As Simmons observes, "it suggests that the gap between the ego and the Other will never be bridged. Awareness of this distance leads to humility and suspension of certainty."[45] The space in between the ego and the other is not just 'nothingness" but a space-a space of alterity. This new imaginative space of *subalternity* and *marginality* is well explained in her notion of *planetarity*.

3. Planetarity

The Spivakian notion of *planetarity*, as in the case of *subalternity* and *marginality*, is a space of *alterity and difference*. In *planetarity*, she elucidates the difference between the notions of globe which is conceptualized in the program of capitalism in the era of globalization and the notion of planet that is conceptualized as a "sheer space of alterity." "I propose the planet to overwrite the globe," Spivak comments. She constructs planetarity as a "limiting idea to counter act the global reach of capital and the computerized globe." In her words: "The globe is on our computers. No one lives there. It allows us to think that we can aim to control it. The planet is in the species of alterity, belonging to another; and yet we inhabit it, on loan."[46] She further says that 'it belongs to another system-a system that is beyond our grasp as it is the inside of our bodies."[47] Ritu Birla explains the notion clearly: "The planet, unlike the world, is a conceptual metaphor infused with the possibility of seeing from outside, of seeing from the perspective of the alien, and not merely of apprehending the unified sphere that is familiar to us from prominent discourses of absolute oversight."[48]

Spivak asserts that the globe on which we live is a manageable world where we are successful and comfortable in showing love to our 'others.' On the other hand, she proposes 'planetary love' which is not love for the other; rather, it is an experience of the 'deconstructive embrace' where both the self and other invent for their new incarnations. Spivak comments that this love is dangerous as it is powerful and it is the *irreducible supplement*.[49] *Planetarity* is a mentality in which we re-visit the constitutive other and the self in the context of globalization and envisage a 'radical relationality' that extends to the whole system of life on the planet. She continues: "if we imagine ourselves as planetary subjects rather than global agents, planetary creatures rather than global entities, alterity remains underived from us. This is as close to the *sacred*, again, as I come."[50]

As Kwok Pui-lan contends, *planetarity* is an invitation to imagine the complexity and plurality of planetary systems and not be confined by narrow identity politics or superficial binary thinking. It is not just an ecological exhortation or a theological/ethical reminder of our stewardship. A planetary ethics thus calls for the experience of the impossible-*detranscendalized sacred*-that is radically open-ended and that is "to come."[51] Instead of God, Spivak here uses the word – 'planet' where we experience the 'detranscendelized sacred' and the 'deconstructive embrace.' It is in this *planetarity* that irreducibility and relationality are affirmed and experienced.

Following Derrida, Spivak does not believe in a religiosity which is opposite to secularity. She doesn't talk about a theology of God. She doesn't believe in a super natural God who is antagonist towards nature. On the other hand, her notion of *detranscendelized sacred* that "aims to destabilize the binarism between secularist politics and the religious practice," alludes to the notion of displaced transcendence or immanent transcendence.[52] According to Spivak, to be attentive to the *detranscendelized sacred* means to live in a 'radical love' –the 'irreducible supplement.'[53] This 'radical love' is not simply an obligation to the 'other' as it is theologized by religions; "love your neighbor" and by human rights activists: "solidarity with the other." It is not just trying to speak for others. Spivak comments that even the slogans like "learning from below" can be a winning slogan in the contemporary context of globalization. She seems to be struggling to signify religion or religiosity, in a globalized secularity, by destabilizing its 'autonomy' and 'otherness' as it is in conventional thinking. Religion, for Spivak, is to live in radical love.

However, for Spivak, *planetarity* is not a license for easy theological talk about the 'the wholly other' or a 'transcendent God.[54] *Planetarity* deconstructs the dichotomy between transcendence and immanence. According to Spivakian planetarity, transcendence is being brought to the mundane, earthly and within space. As Susan Abraham contends, in Spivak transcendence is presented as the going out of self in response to the need of the other.[55] It is an invitation to live in an enigmatic relationship with the other, God and the earth. Here time, space, home, identity, and nature become enigmatic, alluric, and uncanny. The Spivakian *detranscendelized sacred* provides a vision of a relational, embodied, and sensible God that transcends the western, theistic, ontological theology of God. As Jea Sophia Oh argues, Spivakian planetarity comes to us as a call for responsibility. It is not one of romantic imagination but one that reflects the ethical practice of human beings as planetary subjects.[56] Spivak, who signifies the planet as God, defines planetarity as religiosity. Developing this de-ontological Spivakian notion of God, Mayra Rivera proposes a theology of Holy Ghost, through which it is re-imagined as a theological figure that touches us with the haunting memories of human history in terms of the "ghostly encounters" of the victims.[57]

Signifying Spivak for a Postcolonial Political Theology

Postcolonial theologians consider Spivak as one of the most important interlocutors in the contemporary context.[58] It was the Spivakian theorization of the neocolonial Empire that evoked some theologians to de-colonize the western theological imaginations embodied in Christian Theology. The book *Postcolonial Theologies: Divinity and Empire* (2004) was an outcome of this desire. To introduce the book, the editors write: "We use postcolonial theory in ways that commit us to something more than theory-that is, to an engaged and engaging theology, a work of resistance to the layered, ongoing, and novel colonizations of the planet."[59] Stating that Christian theology suffers from an imperial condition, Catherine Keller signifies the imperative to attend to the excluded people-the colonized other-the subaltern and their experiences in the theological program. Keller writes:

> With its [Christian Theology] imperial success, the church, one might argue, absorbed an idolatry of identity: a metaphysical Babel of unity, an identity that homogenizes the multiplicities it absorbs, that either excludes or subordinates every creaturely other, alter, subaltern.[60]

For Keller, one of the most important agendas for postcolonial theology is to interrogate the ontological identity of western theology and its Omni-God. Taking their cue from Spivak, postcolonial theologians focus on the transgressing space of 'in between' or 'interstitial space' in which the power of hegemony is subverted and the colonial other is de-othered. According to Vitor Westhelle, this (non) space is alluring, dynamic and revealing where the subaltern 'preaches' if not speaks.[61]

In order to signify Spivak for a postcolonial theological imagination, Catherine Keller traces Spivak's contentions with liberation theology.[62] According to Spivak, Christian theology does not exceed the "ebb and flow" of the power of Christianity as a 'religion.'[63] She upholds the view that Christianity like any other 'great religion' in the world is imbricated with power. Spivak interrogates the 'other-worldly transcendence' and the 'super-natural thinking' of (western) Christian Theology. At the same time, she acknowledges the role of theology as a resource to engage in social analysis and political practice in the contemporary postcolonial context.[64] While signifying the role played by liberation theologies to envisage an ecologically just world, Spivak seems skeptical about their theological methodology that is based upon 'individual transcendence' (as she calls it). She writes:

> Having seen, then, the powerful yet risky roles played by Christian liberation theology, some of us have dreamt of an animistic liberation theology to girdle perhaps the impossible vision of an ecologically just world. Indeed the name "theology is alien to this thinking. Nature is also super-nature in this way of thinking and knowing... Even super, as in supernatural, is out of the way. For Nature, the sacred other of the human community, is in this thinking, also bound by the structure of ethical responsibility. No individual transcendence theology, of being just in this world in view of the next, however the next is underplayed, can bring us to this.[65]

Spivak shares her desire to have 'liberation without theology.' At this point, Keller raises some questions related to the Spivakian reading of 'animistic liberation theologies' and ecotheologies. Responding to the Spivakian comment on theology that is alien to the thinking of an eco-centric world view, Keller writes: "But, Spivak's perfunctory critique misses the mark."[66] Keller, on the other hand, points out some of the liberationist, Eco/feminist theologies that have emerged in the post-War period that interrogated the dualistic thought of the Western imaginary of the divine and located the notion of transcendence in the materiality of bodiliness. According to Keller, liberation theology in general, especially theologians such as Ivone Gebara, Charles Hartshorne, Grace Jantzen and Sallie McFague, who have approached the universe as the body of God or Divinity as our sacred body, destabilize the other-worldly, super-natural, individual transcendent content of the (western) Christian theology and they represent a chorus of voices about which Spivak seems to be ignorant.

However, some recent studies take a different stand on this point. While discussing the question of mundane transcendence and enmattered subjectivity in eco-feminist theologies, Anne Elvey contends that the assumed asymmetric relationship between God and nature becomes problematic since that sets a 'transcendent Other' outside of the world who is capable enough to come down and touch the earth.[67] For Anne Elvey, even in Rosemary Radford Reuther's theology of 'immanent transcendence,'[68] we sense a 'transcendent God' who embraces the world. This problem is clearly evident in Elizabeth Johnson also. In Johnson's words:

> Distinct from classical theism which separates God and the world, and also different from pantheism which merges God and the world, panentheism holds that the universe, both matter and spirit, is encompassed by the Matrix of the living God in an encircling that generates freedom, self-transcendence, and the future, all in the context of the interconnected whole.[69]

Luke Higgins argues that even in Sallie McFague's theology of creation as the 'body of God' provides room for a pre-eminent spirit:

> In this body model, God would not be transcendent over the universe in the sense of external to or apart from, but would be the source, power, and goal-the spirit-that enlivens (and loves) the entire process and its material forms. The transcendence of God, then, is the pre-eminent or primary spirit of the universe.[70]

While signifying the Spivakian notion of 'detranscendelized sacred' for postcolonial theological thought, Susan Abraham contends that Spivak invokes theology in order to revise its onto-theological and metaphysical framework. Abraham argues that in Spivak the relationship between transcendence and immanence shifts to a material and cultural plane while eschewing identitarian cultural conventions. As Abraham highlights, the problem of sexual difference is not ignored in Spivakian thought of the sacred. As she clearly explicates, in Spivakian thought the transcendence is detranscendelized and brought to the realm of worldly encounters. At the same time, she argues that Spivak's planetary postcolonial thought is not confined to anti-imperial discourse; rather, it goes beyond the so-called identitarian postcolonial theological engagements.

Thus, Spivakian thought locates itself in an uncanny space in between postcolonial, postmodern, and liberation theologies. What is specific is that, in contrast to the (western) Christian theology, the Spivakian detranscendentalized transcendence alludes to an ethico-political theological thought that signifies the immediate, urgent, and present encounters. The Spivakian sacred is encountered in the ethico-political realm of the worldly encounters between the self and the other. The Spivakian notion of sacred or God differentiates itself from the theistic, monotheistic, and ontological theology of the western God. In fact, she would like to celebrate the sad demise of the transcendental God and the notion of the 'absolute Other' whether it is human other or nature. She alludes to an "enmattered God" as in the case of the Deleuzian *chaosmos*. For Deleuze, *chaosmos* is generated "from within" by a wholly immanent process of self-organization.[71] Spivak talks about 'planet' through which she envisages a relational, embodied, and multiple transcendence. Contemporary postcolonial theologians engage with this Spivakian understanding of 'mundane transcendence' in order to re-visit the traditional Christian theology of God, human, and creation.

One of the significant works that appropriates the Spivakian theory of planetarity to formulate a postcolonial theology of God is Mayra Rivera's *The Touch of Transcendence*. Signifying Spivakian planetarity, Rivera offers a model of 'relational transcendence.' She places the question of transcendence in a multiplicity of relations. It is in the flesh of relations that transcendence happens. The space in which the transcendence happens is the site of the intimate embrace, the shared place of our ethical actions, the interval that protects the otherness of the other. For Rivera, "space" evokes images of intrinsic relations between materiality and the transforming energies of life.[72] This 'intermediary space' is not null and void; rather, it is a space that nurtures each one of us. Rivera comments: "it is in this 'space of difference' the needs of the Other touch me."[73] It is the place where we experience the glory of God. She affirms that the glory of God is always encountered as flesh. It is in this 'touch of transcendence' that we experience the glory of God in the flesh of our encounter with the Other. In sum, Spivak becomes an effective interlocutor for a postcolonial theology of God.

Spivakian notion of 'subalternity' signifies a postcolonial imagination of human subjectivity and body. Spivakian subalternity offers a 'third position' of being human other than the self and the other. It signifies a marginal position of 'quite-other.' It is a living position of alterity and deference. It evokes a non-essentialist and non-identitarian social position. It is a political location of de-othering as it denies all kinds of epistemological practices of distancing. It is a rhetorical space of postcoloniality through which all kinds of subjugation are being denied. The Spivakian notion of planetarity alludes to a post-materialistic philosophy of body through which all kinds of hegemonic traces are being resisted. Spivakian planetary love further defines it as an open space for the multiple practices of love other than the love for the other. W. Anne Joh calls this "Love's multiplicity"—the pluralization of love—that envisages a 'counter imperial ecology of love.'[74] This 'counter imperial ecology of love' always affirms the mutuality and the alterity of the human subjectivity. It is a subjectivity of relationality by which humanity is organically connected with the planet earth.

Engaging with Spivakian notion of planetarity, Whitney Bauman proposes a postcolonial theology of creation. Denying the western theology of *creatio ex nihilo* that functions as a foundation for the (western) Christian logic of domination, Bauman proposes a post-colonial theology of God and creation that stem from the notion of the 'beginning' which is 'bio-historical,' 'collective,' and 'interrelated' rather than from 'origin' which is monolithic, absolute and colonial.[75] Alluding to Spivakian planetarity, Bauman proposes a postcolonial theology of *creatio continua* in which creation is not just static or mute; rather, it is 'emergent,' 'gift,' 'open-ended' and 'continuous.' Bauman opines that the 'gift' notion of creation, rather than that of owned property, enables humans to take responsibility for their co-creative nature-cultures.[76] For Bauman, *creatio continua* enables us to have a postcolonial vision of God-earth-human which opens to a kind of responsibility and emerging newness-a notion of planetary citizenship. It is a vision of God who is the creativity of the creation bringing newness to it always. It is a kind of counter understanding of creation that is always open to future, open to difference, and open to change. It is an invitation to live 'in-between' nature and culture, human and nonhuman, self and other, and life and death. In a nutshell, Bauman's postcolonial theology of creation offers us a materialist vision of human subjectivity where God is an internal experience of creativity and transformation.

Conclusion

Skepticism of Spivak about the program of theology, however, provokes it to be 'an ethico-political' responsibility. By de-stabilizing the 'autonomy' and 'the power' inscribed in religions, the Spivakian notions of subalternity, marginality, and planetarity reimagine theology as an act of 'radical relationality' in the world of 'othering.' Christian Theology after Spivak becomes a materialist, secular, political counter-imagination of 'radical love' as it realizes its postcolonial sensitivity. The postcolonial sensitivity of Christian Theology necessitates its internal breaking in terms of its programs of speaking for the margin, with the margin and to the margin; rather asking it to learn to listen to the unspoken voices of the margin. According to Spivak, it is an act of *Teleopoiesis*. Thus, training in the imagination to learn to learn from the subaltern becomes paradigmatic to theological methodologies in the contemporary context.

Spivakian theory of subalternity offers a radical political theology. Spivak reconstitutes the subaltern as the rhetorical space where the ontology of the margin is reconfigured and the epistemology of political practice is reconstructed. Spivakian notion of subaltern invokes us to have a methodology to *learn to learn from the other* while it casts off any notions of essentialism, Identitarianism, worlding and otherisation. Subaltern is neither the object nor the end of political programs: rather it comes as a teacher. The 'truth' of the subaltern agency is differed and fixed at infinity which affirms the 'irreducible singularity' of the subaltern and thus subaltern theology is envisaged as a process of *training in the imagination* by losing one's own privileged positions and see for themselves through the eyes of the other. Thus, subalternity becomes an anarchical point or Eucharistic point for theology to realize its inherent possibility of crucifixion and deconstruction.

Planetarity as a theological imagination offers a notion of a de-transcendentalized sacred. It is a subaltern theology of God who 'empties out' the transcendental baggage of the western colonial imaginary. The subaltern immanent God is an enmattered God who is embodied in the political becoming of subalterns. This is the crucial problem with the subaltern politics in India. The transcendental ethos of Indian political programs either tries to represent the subaltern voices in the public space or quite them by their emancipatory political paradigms. Spivak would rather urge us to learn to listen to the subaltern whose speech is not heard in the power dynamics of the sovereign state. The learning to listen to the subaltern would promote the counter-political process that may even re-constitute the whole imagination of nationality in favour of the subaltern. Of course, it is a kenotic point of social democracy and political practice in India.

End Notes

1 Spivak, *The Post-Colonial Critic: Interviews, Strategies, Dialogues,* ed. Sarah Harasym (New York and London: Routledge, 1990), 83.

2 Ibid.

3 Ibid.

4 Mariam Nandi, *Gayatri Chakravorty Spivak*: 2006: 129 cited by Constanze Lemmerich, *Gayatri Chakravorty Spivak, The Question of Representation of the Subaltern in the Context of Neo-colonialism & Globalization*, Germany: Grin Vertag, 2008), 6.

5 Spivak, *A Critique of Postcolonial Reason: Toward a History of the Vanishing Present* (London: Cambridge, 2003), 52.
6 Donna Landry/Gerard MacLean, eds. Introduction. *The Spivak Reader: Selected Works of Gayatri Chakravorty Spivak* (New York: Routledge, 1996), 4.
7 Landry and MacLean cited by Catarina Kinnavall, Gayatri Chakravorty Spivak, in Jenny Edkins and Nick Vaughan-Williams, *Critical Theorists and International Relations* (London and New York: Routledge, 2009), 318.
8 It is being coined after the Toni Morrison's term 'Dancing Mind.' Toni Morrison, cited by Kwok Pui-lan, "What has Love to Do with It?" in *Planetary Loves*, 32.
9 Stephen Morton, *Gayatri Chakravorty Spivak: Ethics, Subalternity and the Critique of Postcolonial Reason* (London: Polity Press, 2007), 3.
10 Edward Said, *Orientalism* (London: Routledge, 1978), 2.
11 Sumit Chakrabarti, *The Impact of the Postcolonial Theories of Edward Said, Gayatri Spivak, and Homi Bhabha on Western Thought* (Lewiston: The Edwin Mellen Press, 2010), 180.
12 Spivak hesitates to be located as a postcolonialist, even though she is designated as one among the 'Postcolonial Trinity.' Edward Said and Homi Bhabha are the two other most influential exemplars of postcolonial theory. One of the main reasons for this rejection of the label 'postcolonial' is an increasing recognition that postcolonial theory focuses too much on past forms of colonial domination, and is therefore inadequate to criticize the impact of contemporary global economic domination of the economic agencies of the west on the economies and societies of the global South. See for more detailed discussion, Stephen Morton, *Gayatri Chakravorty Spivak: Ethics*, 2.
13 Spivak, *The Post-Colonial Critic*, 104.
14 Spivak, *The Spivak Reader*, 9.
15 Spivak is often called a "feminist-Marxist-deconstructivist"; see MacCabe, Foreword, *In Other Worlds: Essays in Cultural Politics*, (New York and London: Routledge, 1988), ix. However, Spivakian usage of deconstruction is affirmative and thus she calls herself as a 'stain' on the Derridean deconstruction.
16 Sumit Chakrabarti, *The Impact of the Postcolonial Theories of Edward Said*, 180.
17 Mayra Rivera, *The Touch of Transcendence: A Postcolonial Theology of God (London: Westminster John Knox Press, 2007)*, 116.
18 Spivak reads Marx through the lenses of Derridean deconstruction and feminism. The foundationalist approach of Marxism that legitimizes a monolithic reading of social structure and an essentialist social location for the marginalized, provoke Spivak to propose a project of subalternity through which she rescue the marginality from any kind of enclosure. See, Sumit Chakrabarti, *The Impact of the Postcolonial Theories*, 320.
19 Spivak criticizes Marx for holding a unilateral view of the gendered international division of labor that ignores the problem of women. Spivak, *The Post-colonial Critic*, 100.

20 Ibid., 121.
21 Spivak, 'French feminism in an International Frame,' in *In Other Worlds: Essays in Cultural Politics* (New York: Methuen, 1987), 136.
22 Ibid.
23 Spivak, *A Critique of Postcolonial Reason,* 390.
24 Ibid., 386.
25 Moore-Gilbert, *Postcolonial Theory: Contexts, Practices and Politics* (London: Verso, 1997), 92.
26 Ritu Birla, "Postcolonial Studies", in *Can the Subaltern Speak? Reflections on the History of an Idea,* ed. Rosalind C. Morris (New York: Columbia University Press, 2010), 88.
27 Sangeeta Ray, "An Ethics of the Run," cited by Stephen D. Moore, "Situating Spivak" in *Planetary Loves*, 17.
28 *Subaltern Studies Collective* consists of certain historians who aimed to promote a systematic discussion of subaltern themes in South Asian Studies. The group-formed by Ranajit Guha, and initially including Shahid Amin, David Arnold, Partha Chatterjee, David Hardiman and Gyan Pandey-has produced five volumes of *Subaltern Studies: Essays Relating to the History, Politics, Economics and Culture of Subalternity.*
29 For a detailed study of the epistemological trajectories of the category-*subalternity* in the theoretical methodology of the Subaltern Study Collective, see the introductory essay 'A Brief History of Subalternity' in *Reading Subaltern Studies,* ed. David Ludden (Delhi: Permanent Black, 2001), 1-42.
30 Bill Aschroft, Gareth Grifith, and Helen Tiffin, eds., *Key Concepts in Post-colonial Studies* (London: Routledge, 1999), 217 .
31 Spivak, *A Critique of Postcolonial Reason,* 262.
32 Ibid., 273.
33 Spivak, *The Spivak Reader,* 292.
34 Spivak, *A Critique of Postcolonial Reason,* 274.
35 Ibid., 72-74.
36 Spivak, *In Other Worlds,* 205.
37 Spivak, *A Critique of Postcolonial Reason,* 310.
38 Spivak, *The Post-Colonial Critic,*; Stephen D. Moore and Mayra Rivera, eds., *Planetary Loves,* 145-6.
39 According to Spivak, 'Echo' is an attempt to give women a space to deconstruct her out of the representation and non-representation, however imperfectly. See, Spivak, 'Echo,' *The Spivak Reader,* 177.
40 Spivak, *Other Asias* (Oxford: Blackwell, 2008), 17.
41 'Native Informant' is the category which denotes the native people who may be the academicians, politicians, economists or social activists who represent whole native people to the European continent. Sanders Mark, *Gayatri Chakravorty Spivak, Live Theory* (London and New York: Continuum, 2006), 10.

42 Spivak, *The New Subaltern: A Silent Interview*, in *Mapping Subaltern Studies and The Postcolonial*, ed. Vinayak Chaturvedi (London and New York: Verso, 2000), 324-340.
43 Stephen Morton, *Gayatri Chakravorty Spivak*, 60.
44 William Paul Simmons, *Human Rights Law and the Marginalized Other* (New York: Cambridge University Press, 2011), 141.
45 Ibid., 142.
46 Spivak, *Death of Discipline* (New York: Columbia University Press, 2003), 72.
47 According to Spivak, the body is metapsychological where you feel and live in a radical alterity.
48 Ritu Birla, "Postcolonial Studies," 97.
49 Spivak, "Love: A Conversation," in *Planetary Loves: Spivak, Postcoloniality, and Theology*, ed. Stephen D. Moore and Mayra Rivera (New York: Fordham University Press, 2011), 60.
50 Ibid., 62.
51 Kwok Pui-lan, "What has Love to Do with It? Planetarity, feminism, and Theology," in *Planetary Loves*, 33.
52 Susan Abraham, "Detranscendalizing Postcolonial Theology," in *Planetary Loves*, 80.
53 Spivak, "Love: A Conversation," in *Planetary Loves*, 60.
54 Mark Lewis Taylor, "Subalternity and Advocacy as Kairos for Theology," in *Opting for the Margins*, 40-41.
55 Susan Abraham, "The Pterodactyl in the Margins: Detranscendalizing Postcolonial Theology," in *Planetary Loves*, 81.
56 Jea Sophia Oh, *A Postcolonial Theology of Love: Planetarity East and West* (California: Sopher Press, 2011), 81.
57 Mayra Rivera, "Ghostly Encounters: Spirits, Memory, and the Holy Ghost," in *Planetary Loves*, 135.
58 The postcolonial theology that emerged in the mid-1990s began in the field of biblical studies through which the ancient imperial context of the biblical texts and their use in Western colonial adventures were exposed and interrogated. See, Kwok Pui-lan, *Discovering the Bible in the Non-Biblical World* (Maryknoll, N.Y.: Orbis Books, 1995); Laura E. Donaldson and Kwok Pui-lan, eds., *Postcolonialism, Feminism, and Religious Discourse* (London and New York: Routledge, 2002); Kwok Pui-lan, *Postcolonial Imagination and Feminist Theology* (Louisville, Ky.: Westminster John Knox); Kwok Pui-lan et al., eds., *Empire and the Christian Tradition: New Readings of Classical Theologians* (Minneapolis: Fortress Press, 2007); Joerg Rieger, *Christ and Empire* (Minneapolis: Fortress Press, 2007); Stephen D. Moore, *Empire and Apocalypse: Postcolonialism and the New Testament* (Sheffield, UK: Sheffield Phoenix Press, 2006); R. S. Sugirtharajah, ed. *Asian Biblical Hermeneutics and Postcolonialism: Contesting the Interpretations* (Maryknoll, N.Y.: Orbis Books, 1998); R. S. Sugirtharajah, *The Bible and Empire: Postcolonial Explorations*

(Cambridge, UK: Cambridge University Press, 2005), Fernando F. Segovia, *Decolonizing Biblical Studies: A View from the Margins* (Maryknoll, N.Y.: Orbis Books, 2000) Vitor Westhelle, *After Heresy: Colonial Practices and Post-Colonial Theologies* (Oregon: Cascade Books, 2010) are some of the early engagements in postcolonial biblical criticism and theology.

59 Catherine Keller, Michael Nausner, and Mayra Rivera, eds., Preface, *Postcolonial Theologies, Divinity and Empire* (Missouri: Chalice Press, 2004), xi.

60 Catherine Keller, "The Love of Postcolonialism, Theology in the interstices of Empire," in *Postcolonial Theologies, Divinity and Empire*, 223.

61 Vitor Westhelle, *After Heresy: Colonial Practices and Post-Colonial Theologies* (Oregon: Cascade Books, 2010), 147.

62 Catherine Keller, "The Love of Postcolonialism, Theology in the interstices of Empire," in *Post-Colonial Theologies*, 238-242.

63 Spivak, *A Critique of Postcolonial Reason*, 382.

64 Spivak, "Love: A Conversation," in *Planetary Loves*, 71.

65 Spivak, *A Critique of Postcolonial Reason*, 382.

66 Catherine Keller, "The Love of Postcolonialism, Theology in the interstices of Empire," in *Postcolonial Theologies*, 238.

67 Anne Elvey, "Material Elements: The Matter of Women, The Matter of Earth, The Matter of God," in *Post-Christian Feminisms: A Critical Approach*, ed. Lisa Isherwood and Kathleen McPhilips (UK & USA: Ashgate, 2008), 53-69.

68 Rosemary Radford Ruether, "The God of Possibilities: Immanence and Transcendence Rethought," The Brighter Side of Faith: *Concilium: International Journal for Theology* no. 4 (2000), 45-54.

69 Ibid., 50.

70 Luke Higgins, "Toward a Deleuze-Guattarian Micropneumatology of Spirit-Dust," in *Ecospirit: Religions and Philosophies for the Earth*, ed. L. Kearns and C. Keller (New York: Fordham Press, 2007), 253.

71 Deleuze develops an evolutionist idea of creation-*chaosmos*. Gilles Deleuze, *Difference & Repetition*, trans. Paul Patton (New York: Columbia University Press, 1994), 299.

72 Ibid., 130.

73 Ibid., 137.

74 Wonhee Anne Joh, 'Love's Multiplicity: *Jeong* and Spivak's Notes toward Planetary Love.' In *Planetary Loves*, 168-190.

75 Whitney A. Bauman, *Theology, Creation, and Environmental Ethics; From Creatio ex Nihilo to Terra Nullius* (New York, London: Routledge, 2009).

76 Ibid., 164.

3

Messianic Politics and Church Political Theology of Giorgio Agamben

The Italian philosopher Giorgio Agamben is one of the leading figures in philosophy and political theory. His unique readings of literature, literary theory, continental philosophy, political thought, theology, and art have made him one of the most innovative thinkers of our time. In his oeuvres, Agamben exposes the mysterious relationship between theology and politics and thus opens up new vistas of radical political theology. According to Agamben, there is a genealogical conviviality between theology and politics in western philosophy. Taking the cue from Carl Schmitt whose political theology had been widely used for legitimizing the German nationalism, Agamben argues that in the western tradition, understandings of political sovereignty correlate with understandings of divine sovereignty. Analyzing the emergence of the doctrine of Economic Trinity in the early Christian tradition, Agamben contends that Christian Theology through its liturgical practices legitimizes the notion of sovereign power and its governmentality. For Agamben, liturgy reinstates the political activity of the church through which it legitimizes ecclesiastical hierarchy and power. Critiquing modern political theologies for being inadequate to recognize the 'theo-political' project of Christian Theology and the western political philosophy, Agamben, on the other hand, offers impetus for a radical political theology which rejects the liturgical legitimization of the sovereign God and affirms the potential to formulate the anti-imperial subjectivities. This chapter tries to interact with Agamben's political thought for constructing a radical political theology in the contemporary context of neoempire.

Giorgio Agamben: Life and Works

Giorgio Agamben was born in 1942 in Rome. He was educated in law and philosophy at the University of Rome. His doctoral thesis was on the political thought of Simone Weil. He did his post-doctoral studies in Freiburg (1966–1968) where he participated in Martin Heidegger's seminars on Hegel and Heraclitus. Later he became a fellow at the Warburg Institute, University of London, from 1974 to 1975. Agamben then began his long teaching career over the next four decades and taught at the University of Macerata, the University of Verona, the Collège Internationale de Paris, the Università della Svizzera Italiana, the Università Iuav di Venezia, the New School, University in New York and the European Graduate School/EGS where he holds the Baruch Spinoza Chair. Currently, he is the professor of Philosophy and Aesthetics at the University of Verona in Italy. He caused a controversy when he refused to submit to the "biopolitical tattooing" requested by the United States Immigration Department for entry to the USA in the wake of the September 11, 2001 attacks.[1] Agamben considered it as a biopolitical exercise of the sovereign state upon human bodies as it was in the period of Nazi regime.

Agamben is a man of the Left, politically speaking, which means that he was influenced by the promises of the revolutions of 1968, the fall off the Berlin Wall in 1989 and the consequent dissolution of the Soviet Empire. This was a generation of utopian political hopes of a broadly Marxist kind, hopes that had to be re-configured because of the discrediting of standard-issue of Marxist theory. One resource for this reconfiguring is the material preserved in the Christian archive, especially the Pauline material which was most appealing to those post-Marxists. Agamben reads Paul not as a New Testament Scholar; rather he wants to re-read Paul for constructing a sharp critique of the Western political thought on law and subjectivity. Agamben's reading of Pauline universalism and Ekklesia help him to think about the coming community as it theorizes the formation of 'singularities' and de-subjectification.

Agamben's oeuvres engage with wide range of issues relating to language, metaphysics, aesthetics, politics, ethics, liturgy, and theology. One of the enduring concerns of his writings is the critique of sovereign power and its political treatment of human subjectivities. His series of texts known as the 'Homo Sacer' tetralogy explores the above issue and analyzes the figure of the *Muselmanner*—the most degraded and hopeless victims in the Nazi death camps.[2] According to Agamben, this figure who lives in between law and lawlessness, human and in-human, and life and death signifies a crucial state of human life—the 'living dead.' This form of life, which Agamben calls 'bare life' or 'homo sacer' ("sacred man") is the main content of the series of his works, which also includes: *Homo Sacer: Sovereign Power and Bare Life* (1998); *State of Exception* (2005); *The Time That Remains: A Commentary on the Letter to the Romans* (2005); and *Profanations* (2007).

It is well evident in his works that he has been heavily influenced by both the canonical figures of Western political thought from Aristotle, through to Hegel and Nietzsche and the early twentieth century thinkers like Hannah Arendt, Carl Schmitt, Michel Foucault and Walter Benjamin. Alluding to Benjamin, Agamben often uses the theological term "messianic" to describe his argumentative strategy of antinomianism. In order to find a way out of the destructive paradoxes of western legal thought, Agamben frequently draws on messianic texts from the Jewish, Christian, and Islamic traditions. Agamben analyzes the enforcement of rules and the formation of legal subjectivities in the monasteries in his book *The Highest Poverty: Monastic Rules and Form-of-Life* (2013) and warns us to avoid the same pitfalls in our contemporary efforts to find some way to escape the destructive killing machine-the law. Agamben deals with the issue of economy of salvation and its political ramifications in theology and politics vividly in his widely read books *The Kingdom and the Glory: For a Theological Genealogy of Economy and Government* (2007) and *Opus Dei: An Archaeology of Duty* (2013).

Giorgio Agamben and Political Philosophy

Giorgio Agamben's political philosophy intertwines two diverging traditions of philosophical thought: Carl Schmitt's political philosophy and Michael Foucault's biopolitics.[3] Carl Schmitt following Hobbesian notion of sovereignty which is very close to the Christian idea of theocracy, legitimized the sovereignty of the state which in turn supported the Nazi regime in Germany in 1920s. Critically engaging with Carl Schmitt, who defined sovereignty as the power to decide the state of exception where the law is indefinitely suspended without being abrogated, Agamben followed the Foucauldian philosophy of biopolitics where sovereignty inherently legitimizes the state of exception. For Agamben, the state of exception is the inherent phenomenon of the state to provide or deny its legal protection to its citizens. Agamben identifies that the sovereignty of the state is inherently divisive in terms of identifying its citizens who needs to be legally protected and some others as "bare-life"—who live at the state of exception. However, unlike Foucault who identifies the phenomenon of the state of exception with the modern state, Agamben argues that it has existed from the very beginning of sovereignty in the west. Departing from Schmitt and Foucault, Agamben offers a political philosophy of "bare-life"—the people who live at the margins of the state. It is this philosophy of political marginality that makes Agamben significant and crucial in the contemporary context of Empire (Hardt and Negri).

1. The 'Bare-Life'

Taking a look at the ancient Roman law and imperial rule, Agamben argues that the entire history of western political thought (even from the period of Aristotle) bears the horrors of totalitarianism. Tracing the genealogy of the western notion of politics in the early Greek philosophies, Agamben affirms that there is a foundational distinction between natural life (*zoe*) and political life (*bios*).[4] To be a citizen in a polis presupposes a political subjectivity. Agamben asks, then, where is the existence of natural life? He argues that in the notion of sovereignty or the totalitarianism of the state, the natural life (*zoe*) is denied but on the other hand it is presupposed within. No human being is stateless. However, when you fail to become a citizen of the (law) state, according to Agamben, you are automatically becoming a no-human - 'a bearer of life to which anything at all can be done.' Agamben calls this state of life as 'bare-life' or 'state of exception' where certain people live outside the protection of the law of the state (*bios*). The people who live at this 'state of exception' or the 'zone of indistinction', the slaves, the refugees, the inhabitants of the camps, the immigrants, the unborn, the stateless are excluded from the official legal protection and reduced to a state of 'bare-life' where they could be slaughtered, ignored, starved, tortured and imprisoned for life. This exclusion is legally sanctioned and thus they are in a state of 'excluded in' or the 'included out.'[5]

Agamben's analysis of the activity of sovereign power as the production of bare-life in the state of exception (the zone of indistinction) has important implication for the way we think about the politics of space. He explains it:

> Every attempt to rethink the political space of the West must begin with the clear awareness that we no longer know anything of the classical distinction between *zoe* and *bios*, between private life and political existence, between man as a simple living being at home in the house and man's political existence in the city.[6]

Agamben calls this 'zone of indistinction' where 'bare-life' is produced by sovereignty as a form of life camp. The space of the camp, for Agamben, is fundamentally paradoxical. On the one hand, 'the camp is a piece of territory that is placed outside the juridical order.' On the other hand, 'it is not simply an external space.'[7] It is a space of inclusive exclusion. Here exclusion is legally sanctioned. In a camp, the law is suspended and the exceptional practices become the law. Agamben argues that the camp represents: "the most absolute biopolitical space that has ever been realized – a space in which power confronts nothing other than pure biological life without any mediation."[8] For Agamben, camp is not just a historical phenomenon; rather it is "in some sense...the hidden matrix and *nomos* of the political space in which we live."[9] Camp, for him, is "the space that is opened when the state of exception begins to become the rule."[10] In fact he was focusing on the emergence of concentration camps in the late nineteenth centuries in the western world, especially the Auschwitz in Germany and the detention camp at the US Naval Base in Guantanamo Bay.[11]

Agamben argues that there is no natural life (*zoe*) outside of the effect of sovereignty. Alluding to Foucault, Agamben theorizes the biopolitical impact of the sovereignty that forms, reforms and deforms the public life. Thus, life, whether it is biological or political, it is nothing but biopolitical—an act of sovereignty. Agamben identifies a permanent fracture between life and politics in the history of the western political thought which cannot be rectified and thus the political theories, struggles, and manifestoes of the past two and a half millennia become insufficient to reckon with this crisis. It is here that the so-called political theologies are interrogated and challenged. What he tries to communicate is that there is no pure politics to be theorized as a political thought which is detached to the discursive power of the sovereignty. He explains this in *Homo Sacer*:

> Until a completely new politics—that is a politics no longer founded on the exception of bare life—is at hand, every theory and every praxis will remain imprisoned and immobile, and the 'beautiful day' of life will be given citizenship only either through blood and death or in the perfect senselessness to which the society of the spectacle condemns it.[12]

Here Agamben put himself at odd with other political thinkers who hold hope in the contemporary democratic engagements and in the development of a culture of human rights. For him, rights are always connected with nation-states which are inherently sovereign and configure 'zones of indistinction' for refugees.[13] Agamben's sharp criticism with the current political (Human Right) engagement is based on its inadequacy to recognize the problem of the inherent politicization of life—the biopolitics of the sovereign state. For Agamben, it is impossible to get rid of this politicization of life or biopolitics of the sovereign power, and any attempt to resist it will ultimately become an entrenchment of the very powers that is mobilized against. It is here Agamben brings his notion of messianic politics in dialogue with his major interlocutor-Walter Benjamin.

2. Messianic Politics and Church

Alluding to Walter Benjamin, Agamben talks about messianic politics that is founded on the theological notion of the irruption of the messianic time. The state of exception—the bare-life—the living dead—becomes a messianic time of interruption of the sovereignty where the legality of the life is nullified. Agamben here makes use of the Pauline term 'messianic time'—the time that remains—the time that is transfigured in it. It is not a time in between the ascension and *parousia,* rather it is the time that is fulfilled in itself. Agamben here does not theologize the Christian concepts of apocalyptic time or realized eschatology. For Agamben, in those apocalyptical notions there is a *telos,* an *eschaton* that beckons. In Agamben's notion of messianic time, one is invited to be drawn by the *eschaton.* Messianic time, for Agamben, is not one of apocalypse but of Immediacy. Following Benjamin, Agamben affirms that "the paradigm for the understanding of the present is messianic time."[14]

In *The Time that Remains*—an exposition of Romans 1:1-11, Agamben offers an extended discussion on "calling," *kletos,* in the Pauline corpus. He re-reads the opening verse of Roman 1: "Paul, called as slave of Jesus the Messiah..." as the messianic call (*kletos—vocatio* in Latin) to revoke the juridical vocation given by the state. For Agamben, to be called as a slave of Jesus the Messiah is to have a meta-vocation that revokes, or calls back, every other particular vocation like, Jew, gentle, slave, male, female and so on ordered by the state.[15] The *ekklesia,* the community of the called, is then the community of those whose vocations have been revoked but not erased, emptied but not annihilated, removed from the juridical sphere (*bios*) to the bare life (*zoe*). It is a counter-call or call within the call to revoke the biopolitics of the state by creating counter biopolitics (*katargeo*—the deactivation or emptying-out of the law from within). Those who live in *ekklesia* is in the sphere of weakness which alone makes possible the use of their emptied but still present vocations.[16] The church, in the Agamben's political thought, is a community that lives without the law or as outlaws, it is what Agamben likes to call *the coming community*, the community that occupies the time that remains.

According to Agamben, the time that remains is not a slice of time between the ascension and *parousia* of Jesus Christ; rather, it is the time the *ekklesia* takes to come to an end as the time a poem takes to come to an end. This time is a time of transfiguration—the messianic time—the time of the coming community of those whose vocation has been revoked. The eschatology of Agamben is not of the future—end of time (*telos*) but of the present drawn by the *eschaton* (the time of the end). Alluding to Walter Benjamin, Agamben affirms that the paradigm for the understanding of the present is messianic time.[17] Agamben's notion of messianic time offers immediacy and urgency of revocation of our vocations as it is giving back the juridical identity to the state—the giver - and take it back transfigured. It does not deny (of course one can never deny it) the given juridical identity but take it back by transfiguring it. This transfiguration happens in the sphere of coming community which is paradigmatic for public life. For Agamben, this is the messianic politics that begins with us at present, transfiguring our own biological body and the social body.

Church, for Agamben, is the called out community to live for this messianic politics. According to Agamben to be called as a member of Church is to inoperate or de-activate or de-energize the effect of biopolitics of sovereignty and to be baptized by the spirituality of the messianic politics. To be called as a Church means is to become a 'coming community' which lives in the (end) time that remains and to become a non-juridical establishment that runs on certain rules of life. Agamben criticizes the present church for being a juridical institution and thus become empire in this world. Engaging with Paul, Agamben argues that church has become *katoikein* (empire) instead of *paroikein* (sojourn) (1 Peter 1. 17).[18] For him, *Ekklesia* is an ensemble of de-imperialized subjects who live in the messianic time. While defining Church Agamben contends: "Living in this time, experiencing this time, is thus not something that the Church can choose, or choose not, to do. It is only in this time that there is a Church at all."[19] It is this messianic politics that deactivate oneself from the dominant political program and identify with the marginalized and disenfranchised that makes the Church a coming community.

Liturgy and Politics

Tracing the etymological genealogy of the word *leitourgia* in the early Greek philosophy, Agamben tries to expose the epistemological connection between liturgy and politics in the western theological tradition.[20] In the classical Greek culture, *leitourgia* means 'public work' which signifies the obligation that the city (polis) imposes on the citizens who have a certain income to provide a series of services for the common interest. The emperor Constantine exempted clergy from the public services and thus the category-*leitourgia* assumed a cultic sense. Later on, the Alexandrian rabbis legitimized this category as a special cultic category. However, the imperial meaning construction of the term-*leitourgia* is well evident in the subsequent biblical translations especially in the terms like royal priesthood, holy nation etc.[21] Agamben talks about the notion of sacrifice in the book of Hebrews and argues that in this book, Christ is identified as the high priest who sacrifices himself which accomplishes the primordial but unrepeatable liturgical action. For Agamben, "the paradox of Christian liturgy is that by taking the model of its priesthood as the liturgical action of the *archiereus* Christ and founding its authority of the celebrations on the letter to the Hebrews, it devotes itself to repeating an unrepeatable act, to celebrating what cannot be celebrated."[22]

While analyzing the re-configuration of the church (Ecclesia) in the period of early teachers of faith, from the notion of the charismatic community to a juridical organization, Agamben argues that it was the practice of liturgy that substantiated the ecclesiastical hierarchy in its pure juridical framework. The theology of the apostolic succession of the priesthood founded on the notion of the 'royal priesthood of Jesus (Jesus the High Priest) Christ finds its theological substantiation in the concept of *leitourgia.* According to Agamben, *leitourgia* is nothing but a political activity founded on certain theological notions of power and authority. *Leitourgia* provides the sanction to the Church to hold both images: church as a charismatic community and church as a hierarchical organization.[23]

Agamben contends that the definition of the priestly character of the ecclesiastical hierarchy is constructed precisely through founding the sacramental liturgy in the doctrine of Christ as high priest. It is in the theology of the repeatability of the Eucharistic celebration 'forever and ever' that the ecclesiastical hierarchy is also being established 'forever and ever.' The doctrine of the liturgical character of Christ's sacrifice has its root in the doctrine of Trinity itself. Early church fathers defined Trinity as the "economy of mystery" through which they differentiate the ontology and the praxis of God. In this theology of *mysterion* (in Latin *sacramentum*), Agamben argues that, the economic and the political praxis of the church and its priestly action, the mysterious relationship between Christ the high priest and priest the administer, and the celebrant and the recipient are endlessly distinguished and superimposed. Thus through liturgy, church is able to manage to hold both the spiritual and political authority.[24] Agamben argues that the liturgy actualizes the political community between heavenly church and earthly church and at the same time the unity of immanent Trinity and economic Trinity in a sacramental praxis. According to Agamben, the irony with regard to the liturgical theology of the church is that it offers a fake univocity of being and action, liturgy and politics by subordinating the praxis to being and politics to liturgy.[25]

Agamben here tries to reinstate his original thesis: western ontology is totalitarian and sovereign in which economy and politics, liturgy and politics, being and doing are hierarchically integrated and accommodated within. In western tradition, whether it is liturgy or politics, the power of the One-that is sovereign in itself-is being celebrated and dogmatized. Liturgy is nothing but political as it carries out the veneration of the sovereign power. For

Agamben, liturgy is nothing but the practice of "acclamation" 'where the mantle of legitimate sovereignty rests on the shoulders of the people.'[26] As Mitchell Dean explains, "reign, whether it is divine or worldly, is constituted through such (liturgical) practices, and it is they that allow the articulation of the two obligatory poles of power and thereby ensure its operability."[27]

In *The Kingdom and Glory: For a Theological Genealogy of Economy and Government* Agamben argues that the acclamation or the glorification of the angelic hosts is not simply an act of worship but constitutive of both divine and worldly sovereign power.[28] The angelic hosts serve as a model for the hierarchical offices and functions of bureaucracy. Here Agamben's analysis of biopolitics that stems from the Byzantine coronation rituals and acclamations is extended to the modern media and public opinion formation which is operated in the same sense of liturgical ceremoniality of the sovereign power and authority. In a nut shell, Agamben's political thought exposes the operations of political power inherent in the genealogy of Christian theology, liturgy, and politics.

Towards a Political Theology of Immanence

According to the Agamben's political thought, Christianity has to go through a 'catastrophe' in order to experience its 'redemption.' Redemption, for Agamben, is not a future oriented hope; rather it is "in the world as it is, thus." As Renee D. N. van Riessen writes, "redemption is no longer a question of longing for a different, more perfect and thus redeemed world, nor is it the possibility of relating this world in its state of non-redemption to the coming of a redeeming person or event."[29] On the other hand, in Agamben, redemption refers to the possibility of seeing the world at the same time from the perspective of its 'being thus' and of its unfulfilled promises. Thus, Agamben's political thought recommends concentrating on the present and its unfulfilled promises. Church as a coming community is provoked by the political thought of Agamben to be a possible community-a community that is always in the process of coming, becoming a non-juridical community, and embodying the state of exception here in the present but its potential has not yet been grasped. However, Agamben is hopeful that church as a called out community is capable enough to recognize its potentiality through its messianic political practices where the contemporary socio-political and economic sovereign powers surely cannot remain the same. It is in this messianic politics of the church-the coming community, that Agamben entrusts a radical political theology of Immanence.

According to Agamben's radical theology, God cannot be a sovereign-transcendent power. It is an immanent God. The notion of transcendence is not at all rejected in this notion of immanence; rather it is located within the possibility of the messianic irruption within it. It is here that Agamben departs from the Christian political theologians. For Christian political theologies, the immanent political realm is linked to a Transcendent Other God who is supposed to come from outside—Agamben calls it the 'providential' understanding of the Oikonomia.[30] Whereas Agamben argues that it is through this transcendental logic that the capitalist-market discourses serve the role of liturgy today. Today the liturgical or the 'operation of glorification' is well performed by media as public praxis in the contemporary liberal world economy. Breaking of this liturgical continuity of biopolitics and partaking of the messianic politics is the function of the radical political theology of immanence.

Agamben's theology of immanence does not exclude the possibility of transcendence altogether. Immanence, in this sense, takes a 'pure' form of messianic politics. It is a politics of pure immanence, as Agamben explains, that is present within every thought, as the "not external outside" and as the "non-internal inside."[31] In this pure immanence the notion of transcendent God is re-imagined and located within the immanence. Alluding to Wittgenstein, Agamben argues that God is not revealed "in" the world, but the world itself, as it is thus, and insofar as it is absolutely and irreparably profane, is God.[32] God is in the "being thus" of things. Agamben interprets this "being thus" as to be exposed, abandoned and without shelter. God, in Agamben, is the profanatory potential that resides within the realm of 'pure immanence'—the "being thus" of things.

For Agamben, the messianic politics is not a mega (universal) resistance based on the generalized principles such as human rights; rather, it is "to explore and invent the profanatory potential that resides within remnants of forms of subjectification and de-subjectification produced by sovereign power itself."[33] It is the micro politics of de-activating or inoperating the biopolitics of sovereignty within our biological and social bodies and thereby envision new politics and new life. Agamben makes this clear in *Means Without End*:

> It is by starting from this uncertain terrain and from this opaque zone of indistinction that today we must once again find the path of another politics, of another body, of another world. I would not feel up to forgoing this indistinction of public and private, of biological body and body politic, of *zoe* and *bio*, for any reason whatsoever. It is here that I must find my space once again—here or nowhere else. Only a politics that starts from such an awareness can interest me.[34]

Agamben's project of messianic politics is well-evident in his expression 'whatever being.' For him, 'the simple fact of one's own being (existence) is the possibility or potentiality to de-activate sovereignty. The 'whatever beings', is the "singularities" without affirming identity, form the coming community where 'humans co-belong without any representable condition of belonging.'[35] Agamben defines church as the coming community that envisages messianic politics to expose the 'time that remains,' and experiences the state of exception—the experience of the bare-life—the excluded in and the included out here and now. It is the enforcement of this messianic politics that re-orient the church as redemptive and life-giving in the contemporary world of 'repressed sovereignties.'

Conclusion

Agamben points towards the imperative of a radical political thought and practice that would enhance the human life to be escaped out of the hold of sovereign power. The major significance of his radical political thought lies in the demand for the deconstruction of the genealogy of the biopolitics and the fixing up of the location of the radical political thought in the question of 'bare-life' or the 'state of exception' or the natural life 'excluded in'/ 'included out.' It is here that the current political thoughts are being invoked to re-imagine themselves and re-configure its philosophical framework in a postcolonial context. Analyzing the genealogy of kingdom and its glory in the theological tradition of western Christianity, Agamben argues that there has always been a mysterious relationship between liturgy and politics in Christian theology. Agamben exposes the inherent dichotomy between being and doing of God in the early church understanding of economic trinity. For Agamben, it was this theology of economic trinity that promulgated the ecclesiastical hierarchy and the theological notion of the sovereign power/God and thus shaped church into an empire in this world. Signifying a radical theology of immanence, Agamben defines Church as a coming community through which it becomes an embodiment of messianic politics. In Agamben's perspective, liturgy becomes significant when it celebrates the politicality, poeticality, and potentiality of the tortured body-the crucified body of God. As Mark Lewis Taylor rightly contends, 'it is here theology becomes "theological" which is located within the "weight of the world."'[36]

End Notes

1 Mathew Calarco and Steven Decaroli, eds., *Giorgio Agamben: Sovereignty and Life* (Stanford, CA: Stanford University Press, 2007), 9.

2 Justin Clemens, Nicholas Heron and Alex Marray, eds., *The Work of Giorgio Agamben: Law, Literature, Life* (Edinburgh: Edinburgh University Press, 2008).

3 Federico Luisetti, "Carl Schmitt and Giorgio Agamben: From Biopolitics to Political Romanticism," *Journal of Philosophy of Life*, Vol. 1, No. 1 March 2011), 49-58.

4 It was Aristotle who offered the political theory first in west that deals with two different realms of lie: biological (*zoe*) and political (*bios*).

5 A detailed discussion on this theme can be seen in Adam Kotsko, How to Read Agamben http://lareveiw of books.org.

6 Giorgio Agamben, *Homo Sacer: Sovereign Power and Bare Life*, trans. Daniel Heller-Roazen (Stanford: Stanford University Press, 1998), 187.

7 Giorgio Agamben, *Means Without End: Notes on Politics, trans by Vincenzo Binetti and Cesare Casarino* (Minneapolis & London: University of Minnesota, 2000), 40.

8 Ibid., 41.

9 Ibid., 40.
10 Giorgio Agamben *Homo Sacer: Sovereign Power and Bare Life*, 168-9.
11 Auschwitz is the physical manifestation of the Agamben's notion of the camp. Agamben resolutely refuses to refer to the destruction of the Jews in the death camps as a 'holocaust' (etymologically means 'burnt offering') because that unacceptably assimilates the crematoria to the sacrificial alter. Edwin Bikundo, Book Reviews in *Griffith Law Review* (2013) Vol. 22, No. 2.
12 Giorgio Agamben, *Homo Sacer: Sovereign Power and Bare Life*, 11.
13 Giorgio Agamben, "Beyond Human Rights," Open 2008/ No. 15/ *Social Engineering.*
14 Giorgio Agamben, *The Church and the Kingdom,* trans. Leland de Durantaye (London, New York, Calcutta: Seagull Books, 2012), 59.
15 Giorgio Agamben, *The Time That Remains: A Commentary on the Letter to the Romans*, trans. Patricia Dailey (Stanford, CA: Stanford University press, 2013), 11.
16 Ibid., 12.
17 Giorgio Agamben, *the Church and the Kingdom,* 59.
18 Ibid., 2.
19 Ibid., 26.
20 Giorgio Agamben, *The Highest Poverty: Monastic Rules and Form of Life,* trans. Adam Kotsko (Stanford, CA: Stanford University press, 2013), 84.
21 Giorgio Agamben, *Opus Dei: An Archeology*, Trans. Adam Kotsko (Stanford, CA: Stanford University press, 2013), 1.
22 Ibid., 8-9.
23 Ibid., 13.
24 Ibid., 17.
25 Ibid., 18.
26 Alexander Barker, "The Invisible hand," in The *Oxonian Review-* http:/www.oxonianreview.org/wp.
27 Mitchell Dean, "Governmentality Meets Theology: 'The King Reigns, but He Does Not Govern," *Theory Culture Society* 2012 29:145.
28 Giorgio Agamben, *The Kingdom and Glory: For a Theological Genealogy of Economy and Governance*, trans. Lorenzo Chiesa and Matteo Mandarini (Stanford, CA: Stanford University press, 2013), 144.
29 Renee D. N. van Riessen, "Community and its Other, Remarks on Giorgio Agamben's The Coming Community from Levinasian point of view," *Zeitschrift fur DialektischeTheologie,* Supplement Series, 5.
30 Giorgio Agamben, *The Kingdom and Glory,* 314.
31 Giorgio Agamben, *Potentialities: Collected Essays in Philosophy,* trans. Daniel Heller-Roazen (Stanford: Stanford University Press, 1998), 228.
32 Giorgio Agamben, The Coming Community, trans. Michael Hardt (Minneapolis: University of Minnesota Press, 1993), 90.

33 Nick Vaughan-Williams, "Giorgio Agamben," in *Critical Theorists and International Relations,* edited by Jenny Edkins and Nick Vaughan-Williams (London and New York: Routledge, 2009), 28.

34 Giorgio Agamben, *Means Without End,* 139.

35 Giorgio Agamben, The Coming Community, 86; Rene ten Bose, "Giorgio Agamben and the Community without Identity," *Sociological Review,* November 2005.

36 Mark Lewis Taylor, *The Theological and the Political, On the Weight of the World* (Minneapolis: Fortress Press, 2010), 10.

4

Religion as the Ethico-Political Practice of Justice
Political Theology after Ambedkar

As in the case of Agamben, Ambedkar exposes the hegemonic epistemological foundation of the Indian socio-political order which excludes certain sections of people in the account of the social practice—caste, that is legitimized by certain elitist epistemologies and theologies. It was Ambedkar who envisioned caste as a critical social analytical method to investigate the exclusive social order in India and thereby re-instate the excluded people into the social setting reconfigured by the colonial modernity. Being an interlocutor of colonial modernity, Ambedkar explored the possibility of democratizing of the Indian social order on the basis of the socio-political and religious morality which is rooted in the fusion of both Indian and western materialist philosophical discourses.[1] Hence, Ambedkar's political thought remains unique in its alchemy of the materialist philosophical foundation while configuring it in a counter religious—theological framework for exploring the multiplex inhabitations within the colonial modernity. This chapter explores the possibility of constructing a subaltern political theology of Ambedkar by re-reading his political philosophy while allowing him to interact with the other post-continental political thinkers.

A brief Life-Sketch of B. R. Ambedkar

Bhimrao Ramji Ambedkar otherwise known as Babasaheb Ambedkar was born on 14th April 1891 in the military cantonment of Mhow in the central provinces (now in Madhya Pradesh). He was the 14th and the last child of Ramji Maloji Sakpal, an army officer who held the rank of subedar and Bhimabai Sakpal. His family was of Marathi background from the town of Ambadawe in Ratnagiri district of modern-day Maharashtra. Ambedkar was born into a Mahar caste which was one of the untouchable castes in India. As a Mahar boy Ambedkar went through severe experiences of segregation and discrimination in his school days. In 1897, he enrolled at Elphinstone High School, Bombay, for his post-secondary education. Shortly before his matriculation, Ambedkar was married to Ramabai Walangkar from Konkani Mahar family. In 1912 he obtained his degree in economics and political science from Bombay University and in 1913 he moved to Columbia University, USA for his postgraduate studies. In 1916 Ambedkar enrolled at the London School of Economics from where he received his doctorate. Ambedkar was influenced by John Dewey and his work on democracy during his studies at the Columbia University that invoked him to think about a subaltern political practice in India.[2]

After his education, Ambedkar continued his social engagement as an economist, academician and politician. Ambedkar initiated untouchable movement through which he intended to educate and empower dalits to elevate their social dignity and social agency. As Eleanor Zelliot rightly contends, Ambedkar stressed the modernization of dalits and their political rights through conferences, newspapers and organizations.[3] Ambedkar initiated social movements like Temple Entry Movement to organize dalits to recapture their right to enter into the public spaces and use the public resources. It was intended to unite dalits who were disintegrated and scattered for many reasons. In 1936 he founded the Independent Labor Party which contested the 1937

Bombay election to the Central Legislative Assembly. He published *Annihilation of Caste* in 1936 in which he strongly criticized the Hindu-Brahmanic teachings that reinforced and legitimized caste practices. Ambedkar served on the defense advisory committee and the Viceroy's Executive Council as Minister for Labor. In 1947 the new Congress-led government invited Ambedkar to serve as the nation's first Law Minister and appointed him as the chairman of the Constitution Drafting Committee to write Indian's new constitution. In 1955 he founded the Bharatiya Bauddha Mahasabha and completed his final book *The Buddha and His Dhamma.* Ambedkar embraced Buddhism in 1956, two months before his death.

The Thought-World of Ambedkar

Ambedkar appears to be a postcolonial interlocutor of the colonial modernity. The term 'colonial modernity' generally signifies the impact of the European culture in its colonies. The concept of colonial modernity helps us to signify the interstitial spaces in between the colonizer and the colonized.[4] Ambedkar investigated the multiple habitations within the colonial modernity in order to resist both internal and external colonialisms. His major focus was to search for a reconfigured modern identity of the untouchables in the British colonial India where Indian Brahmanic system upheld its power and authority. He approached colonial modernity as a possibility to dismantle the Brahmanical hierarchy that excludes dalits as untouchables while recognizing the inadequacy of the western political liberalism to redeem the victims of the age-old casteism. Locating him at the interstitial space between both colonialisms, Ambedkar envisaged a political space of negotiation for the untouchables who never exercised their agency and identity in the Indian nationhood. This section investigates Ambedkar's epistemological itinerary out of which he configures his subaltern political philosophy.

1. Deweyan Pragmatism and the Modern Liberal Views

It was the influence of the Deweyan pragmatism (John Dewey was his teacher in Columbia University, New York) that inspired

Ambedkar to develop a modern political philosophy in favour of the untouchables and the marginalized in Indian colonial context. However, Ambedkar takes a departure from the notion of the universality of the western enlightenment ideals such as liberty and freedom, and initiates a search for social morality and ethics founded on Indian materialistic philosophies and religious traditions. Realizing the limitation of the notion of universal humanism and its epistemological foundation in the euro-centric rationalism, Ambedkar, on the other hand, explores the possibility of developing counter social ethics from the materialist religious and philosophical traditions like Buddhism. It is here Ambedkar takes a turn from the Habermasian communicative theory that presupposes the universality of reason and the formation of liberal subjectivity. Of course, Ambedkar appropriates the liberal-scientific thinking of the western enlightenment as it is in the Deweyan pragmatism, but that is to challenge the irrational Brahmanic-Hindu knowledges and practices and to modernize Indian society.[5] In nut shell, Ambedkar's subaltern political thought opens up a dialogical epistemological space within colonial modernity which appropriated the indigenous knowledges of social morality and politics in the wider frame work of modern liberal-scientific cultural values.

2. Marxian Influence on Ambedkar

Another important discipline that Ambedkar engages with is Marxism. In his 1961 Columbia essay, 'Castes in India' describes caste as an 'enclosed class.' According to Ambedkar it is the 'enclosure of class' which gives caste its social coherence. Ambedkar uses the word class as a collectivity formed around shared interest and the experience of exploitation. His use of the term *Dalit varga* (class) is to signify the governmental category of depressed classes through which he meant for a dalit political subjectivity in the modern context. Ambedkar-Marxist dialogue intensified during the formation of the Independent labor party on 15 August 1936. Ambedkar used the category labor as an inclusive category of depressed classes. Society is classified into various classes and the depressed classes constitute the excluded-the marginalized. They are excluded from all kinds of ownership, management, and production due to their caste location.

Ambedkar brought caste as a crucial factor in defining the category-labor which is nothing but Ambedkar's "interwar engagement with Marxism."[6] While signifying Ambedkar's emphasis on caste in Indian socio-political context, Anupama Rao clearly analyzes the inadequacy of the Marxist definition of the category-labor in India. Rao contends:

> Labor was thus *underspecified and overdescribed:* it was an organizational element in union activism, a category on whose behalf the Communist Party spoke, and a key category of governance and legal regulation shaped by the joint requirements of industrial capital and the resistances of strike action."[7]

Ambedkar-Marx engagement ultimately led to a postcolonial translation of Marxism which differentiates themselves in their notions of power, body, and capital. Ambedkar contradicts with the Marxist theory of labor and argues that in Indian context the labor of the untouchables has no 'value' or 'count' because it is already defined as defiled and impure. According to Rao, in Ambedkar-Marx dialogue the problem that involves the collision of two kinds of body history, of the body as value, and the body as dispossessed and disposable.[8] In the Brahmanic Hindu social knowledge, the history of labor was embedded in the theory of duty, *varnadsramadharma,* the labor of the *shudra* was *seva*-the service to the social body. Taking the cue from the Vedic epistemology, Gandhi defined labor as a social gift-sacrifice for the social order. For Gandhi service is a 'giving without return."[9] Gandhi's political philosophy of non-violence was in fact inherently violent. For Ambedkar, the primary step for the untouchables is to challenge the stigma embodied on their bodies and to become 'valuable' bodies before making available themselves for emancipation through labor as Marx proposed. Ambedkar wanted dalits to upgrade their subjectivity through modern jobs that he called "counter-revolution in India." His work on *The Buddha or Karl Marx* still remains incomplete.

3. Ambedkar's Engagement with Buddha

Along with Marx, Ambedkar initiates a lifelong interaction with Buddha. Unlike Nagarjuna who takes a mystic turn with Buddhism, Ambedkar takes a secular-political turn with Buddhism.[10] Ambedkar engages with Buddhism through Marx. Differently said, Ambedkar envisages a new form of Buddhism (Navayana Buddhism) with the help of Marx. Ambedkar re-interpreted Buddhism as a morality-centric Dhamma. Buddhism, in its original form, is a heterodox philosophy that denies the Vedic philosophy of God, soul, and karma. Ambedkar denies the philosophy of Hinduism which is impotent to offer an open and free subjectivity and social life based on liberty and fraternity. As Kancha Illaiah writes, Ambedkar re-constitutes Buddhism by defining God as a political philosopher and human-self as futurist and becoming through political engagements.[11] Gail Omvedt clearly states that it is the question of commitment to an egalitarian society that led Ambedkar to approach Buddhism which hails from an anti-hegemonic epistemological standpoint.[12] Thus, in Ambedkar's political thought religion takes a political turn and becomes 'religion after religion.'

While reading Ambedkar's *The Buddha and His Dhamma,* Raosaheb Kasbe rightly analyzes that Ambedkar's Buddha is not just the traditional Buddha; but a Marx-like Buddha.[13] Buddha, for Ambedkar, is a political philosopher who stands for a democratic form of governmentality as it is theorized by Marx. His admiration for Buddha is well-evident in these words:

> As to dictatorship the Buddha would have none of it. He was born a democrat and he died a democrat. At the time he lived there 14 monarchical states and 4 republics. He belonged to the Sakyas and the Sakyas' kingdom was a republic. He was extremely in love with Vaishali which was his second home because it was a republic.[14]

However, Ambedkar-Marx-Buddha dialogue is internally complex and contested one. Ambedkar asks "Could the Buddha answer Karl Marx?" Ambedkar wanted Buddha to answer the questions raised by Marx. By critiquing Marx for the inadequacy of his economic theory and the theory of historical materialism in Indian context, Ambedkar looks into the social formation of the economic-political system that is epistemologically located in the 'pure materialistic' philosophies like *Lokayata.* Ambedkar finds epistemological validity to fulfill the Marxist vision of classless society in the Buddhist Dhamma which further needed to be reconstructed to be a postcolonial political philosophy of casteless society. The epistemological itinerary of Ambedkar's becomes unique in its inter-disciplinary and inter-continental approach. In short, the epistemological itinerary of Ambedkar's political thought locates itself in a locus of Dewey-Marx-Buddha which is internally complicated, contested and disputed.

Political Philosophy of Ambedkar

Ambedkar's political philosophy is analyzed here in three focuses: (1) social precedes political; (2) ethical and religious contents of political philosophy; (3) constitutional democracy and the agency of law.

1. Social Precedes Political

Ambedkar becomes the most prominent political philosopher in the Indian political thought, based on his political theorization of the problem of exclusion. According to Ambedkar there is a permanent inconsistency in the political knowledge of Indian social order. Some sections of people are permanently excluded and their struggle to enter into the political domain constitutes democracy in India inherently problematic. In this contested political situation, Ambedkar comes up with a new slogan: the social precedes political.[15] According to Ambedkar, it is the social content of democracy that enhances the excluded one's struggles to reorganize the social-political order. It is not just the lack of the political conscience, but lack of the moral conscience that becomes important in the Indian context of caste exclusion. Here Ambedkar offers a radical 'punch' to the political philosophy which is internally destabilized and re-defined in terms of the social morality and social democracy.

Kesava Kumar opines that the core of the political thought of Ambedkar is constituted by two assumptions: "the rights are protected not by law but by social and moral conscience of society, and a democratic form of government presupposes a democratic form of society."[16] Unlike the Western tradition of democracy, in Ambedkar's thought democracy is a form of society, or a mode of associated living, and a social consciousness which is founded on high values of morality. For Ambedkar the political democracy presupposes a social democracy. Social democracy presupposes a quality life based on social values of freedom, liberty, and justice. According to Ambedkar, a democratic government means a democratic social structure that brings revolution to the socio-political and economic life of the common people without bloodshed. Here Ambedkar poses the potentiality to annihilate caste as the major criteria to judge the fecundity of a political theory or political practice in Indian context.

2. Ethical and Religious Contents of Political Philosophy

Another significant specialty of the political thought of Ambedkar is that it is primarily ethical and religious in content and practice. According to Ambedkar, Indian social order which is fundamentally built on the caste epistemology of the Vedic religiosity, is to be destabilized and denied on the basis of the modern ideals of democracy, justice and liberty. The moral standard of the Vedic religiosity is not at all acceptable due to its exclusivist and enslaving theology. The authoritarian Hindu social order delimits the freedom and enslaves the majority of the Indian polity. The victims of the caste system are thrown out of the socio-political and economic capitals of the society. Thus, the social order is to be reconstituted on the basis of equality, justice and the moral religiosity. Hinduism is not capable enough to provide an ethical social life due to its caste epistemology. Once he said: "To remain in Hinduism and to attempt to abolish caste system is like sweetening Poison."[17] For him there is no hope for dalits in Hinduism. It is here Ambedkar brings the question of religious conversion as political strategy for freedom and social democracy.

Religion for Ambedkar is nothing but a political community that gives a collective identity to the marginalized people in India. Especially the modern Indian context of nation-state necessitates a collective political identity that is rooted in a religious identity. In the nation-state politics, it is the religious collective identity that signifies the representation of plural sections of people. Analyzing this consciously, Ambedkar argues for a religious identity for the caste victims to be represented in the nation-state political power. Thus, the notion of community becomes central to Ambedkar's political thought. For him, Hinduism is not qualified to be a just community. Islam and Christianity, though they stand for egalitarianism, are politically impotent to challenge the caste epistemology and its practices in Indian context. For Ambedkar, Buddhism has the inherent potentiality to be a moral community based on political reasoning and ethics.[18] Buddhism, unlike Islam and Christianity, has had the history of challenging the caste epistemology theologically and politically. Contrary to the Marxist notion of class, Ambedkar's ideal community is to be created through the moral transformation of an individual from the caste status to the political subjectivity. Ambedkar believes that Buddhism has the potential to initiate this moral transformation because of its anti-casteist epistemological heritage and the moral philosophy of political becoming through *Sangh*.

3. Constitutional Democracy and the Agency of the Law

Ambedkar's political philosophy is marked by its basis on the constitutional democracy and the agency of the law. Ambedkar's engagement with the British government was to ensure the self – representability of the disadvantaged people in the politic discourses of the state. If the untouchables are not represented in the political process, that state becomes sectarian and exclusive. Here Ambedkar exposes the assumption of the Western notion of state that it represents all citizens irrespective of their social locations.[19] The Western notion of the state always functions in the assumption that the excluded are to be incorporated into the mainstream through its emancipatory projects and thereby the state can become politically neutral.

Contrary to the Western notion of the state, Ambedkar destabilizes the notion of the neutrality of constitution of the state and reconfigured it in terms of the multiple locations of its citizens on the basis of a constitutional democracy and the agency of the law.

Ambedkar focuses on the political inclusion of the excluded through the constitutional spacing and the agency of laws and thereby the very constitution of the notion of the state itself can be re-imagined and re-configured. It is here that Ambedkar differentiates himself with the so called 'nationalists' and becomes an 'anarchist.' It is this 'anarchist' position of Ambedkar which enforces the 'nationalist wing' like Indian National Congress and BJP-Sangh Parivar-Hindutva allies to call Ambedkar 'anti-nationalist.' In fact, in this position, the 'nationalist wing' becomes pro-colonial and promoters of colonial modernity.

However, towards the end of his career and political life, Ambedkar comes to the understanding that there is a limitation to the fulfillment of the social democracy and the annihilation of caste through the legal means. Ambedkar stated on All India Radio in 1954: "I deem the place of law very low; because I am not confident to say that law would certainly be of any help with regard to violation of liberty and equality."[20] Thus, Ambedkar moves towards the social role of religion in functioning of a social democracy. J. Soske rightly says that 'Ambedkar moved away from his expanded ideal of state-driven transformation not because he rejected its presuppositions: many of them reappeared in his advocacy of Buddhism as a civic religion.'[21] Of course, in the law's place, he advocated the criterion of a new socio-cultural-political community as the power capable of producing social consciousness and a shared moral order. Conversion to Buddhism was a political agenda of Ambedkar to envisage a political community, political practice and a political theology that challenge the casteist social order and promote political subjectivity to the disenfranchised in the Indian context.

Ambedkar and the Continental Political Philosophy

Continental philosophy as a post-enlightenment Western thought emerges out of the crisis of Western liberalism. In the modern world dominated by Europe, liberalism has functioned to support both economic capitalism and political democracy. The political democracy that continues to support neoliberal capitalism encountered severe criticism from the post-continental philosophers for being authoritarian and sovereign.[22] The concept of sovereignty embedded in the modern political democracy has been severely criticized by Giorgio Agamben's political theory of 'state of exception.' According to Agamben, there are some people who live in the 'state of exception'—'the living dead'—that destabilizes the notion of the sovereignty of the state. Interrogating the notion of sovereign state, Jacques Derrida proposes the theory of 'democracy to-come' that invokes a constant deconstruction of the political process in order to envisage an ever differing meaning of democracy and political subjectivity. Hardt and Negri, on the other hand, come up with the notion of 'multitude' that signifies the political power of the common people as it is opposed to the notion of sovereignty in a post-liberal and postcolonial democratic political process.

Following Foucault's theory of bio-politics, Agamben highlights the inability of the force of law to deconstruct the social body from the discursive formulation of the sovereignty. Here Agamben explains the crisis of the Western political philosophy as it finds difficulty to reconfigure social order out of its liberal, individualistic, rational and sovereign political epistemological framework. Gilles Deleuze tries to address this crisis by fixing it with his theory of 'event.' Deleuze talks about an unconscious event through which we dream for the force of law beyond the law. The problem with these Western political thoughts is that they are founded on certain psychoanalytic ideas and literary aesthetics, rather than political engagements of the marginalized people. It is here that Ambedkar's political philosophy remains significant and different for a postcolonial political thought. Ambedkar's political thought is rooted in the political engagements of the excluded as they take on the hegemonic notions of political power and social order. It is located in the ethical and religious values rather than psychoanalytic ideas and liberal values of capitalism. Unlike the Continental political philosophy, Ambedkar's political philosophy is located in the political becoming of the subaltern subjectivity as they struggle to construct a polyphonic democracy based on the indigenous materialistic philosophies and the heterodox religious traditions. However, in the contemporary context of corporate capitalism, Ambedkar needs to be engaged with those post-continental philosophies in order to envisage a global network of all victims and the affected.

Dhamma: Religion after Ambedkar

Following the Navayana Buddhist philosophy, Ambedkar defines religion as a political philosophy of Dhamma—the ethico-political practice of Justice. He distinguishes between religion and Dhamma. For him, religion is personal whereas Dhamma is social. According to Ambedkar, Hinduism as a reformed Brahmanic philosophy, is ritualistic and thus forms enslaving subjectivities. On the other hand, Dhamma stands for righteousness which means right relationship with all. Dhamma necessitates socio-political relationship and vice versa. Society cannot do without Dhamma. Dhamma leads to liberty and justice. Dhamma consists of *prajna* (reason) and *karuna* (compassion). It is the understanding with compassion and ethics which keeps our social life righteous and democratic.[23] Following Buddha, Ambedkar held the view that religion is connected with revealing the beginning of things or the origin of the world whereas Dhamma is to reconstruct the world. Dhamma is founded on morality and thus it is built on immanence while religion is founded on transcendence. For religion, morality is an attachment since it is linked with the notion of a 'beyond' God; whereas as in Dhamma, the morality takes the place of God, although there is no God in Dhamma. Morality in Dhamma does not need any divine sanction or legitimization from beyond. It arises out of the human relationship for liberty, freedom and justice that is envisaged in the political philosophy of Dhamma.

Morality in Dhamma is considered as sacred because it stands for the protection of the weak. Survival of the weakest is the social imperative behind the morality. It is the morality or the politics of the survival of the weakest that determines the sacrality of the socio-political life. Sacredness is neither beyond the socio-political life nor it substantiates any hierarchical social order within. Unlike religion, Dhamma is not controlled by ceremonies, rituals and liturgies, rather by social morality that sustains the society sacred. For Ambedkar, Dhamma is not just rhetorical, rather it is practical and thus internally political. It is our effort to make our society more ethical and moral that determines the divine content of the social life. God is not regarded as a legitimizing point: rather it is the ultimate ethos of responsibility that invokes us always to strive for a just-moral community. For Ambedkar, the transformation of the society is not linked with any transcendental logic: rather it is embodied in the political formation of the just relationships. It is here that Ambedkar's political theology of (no) God finds semblance with the argument of Giorgio Agamben when he says "God is not revealed "in" the world, but the world itself, as it is thus, and insofar as it is absolutely and irreparably profane, is God."[24] God as the divine potentiality is in the "being thus" of things which is materialist in content. Ambedkar's political philosophy of (no) God provokes Christian theology to seek for an embodied, enfleshed, and enmattered God who is the "being thus" of all political practices of justice, freedom and equality.

Critiquing Christianity as the Religion of Transcendence

Despite of its egalitarianism, Ambedkar is skeptic about the potentiality and the usefulness of Christian theology in challenging the caste knowledges and its practices. According to Ambedkar, Christianity is purely spiritual and transcendental. For him, Christian spirituality is unrelated to the material life and thus it is politically unproductive for the marginalized. Ambedkar argues that it is evident in the life of the dalits who converted to Christianity. The Christian converted Dalits, in Ambedkar's perspective, become apolitical and inactive due to the transcendent content of the Christian doctrines. Analyzing the missionized theology in India, Ambedkar tries to expose the theological inconsistency within the doctrinal discourses of Christian missionary program:

> Instead of being taught that their fall was due to a wrong social and religious environment and that for their environment they must attack the environment, they were taught their fall was due to their sin. Consequently, the Dalit Christians instead of being empowered to conquer their environmental context, conferred themselves with the belief that there is no use of struggling, for the simple reason that their fall is due

> to the sin committed not by them but by some remote ancestors of their called Adam and Eve.[25]

According to James Massey, here Ambedkar stresses that when a dalit Christian "was a Hindu his fall was due to his *karma*. When he becomes a Christian he learns that his fall is due to the sins of his ancestor. In either case, there is no escape for him."[26] In Ambedkar's political philosophy, the transcendental framework of Christianity is being strongly interrogated and the Christian theology is being invoked to deconstruct its doctrinal fecundity in a postcolonial political content. It is well evident in his response: "To teach that Christians have an obligation to love others is no doubt very valuable. But, to stop there and argue that spiritual life expressed in a social attitude is quite unrelated to material life and Christians can have nothing to do with it, is in my judgment to preach an empty doctrine."[27]

Signifying Ambedkar for a Radical Political Theology in India

In the contemporary Indian political context where Hindutva ideology/ political philosophy of the orthodox Hinduism with the support of the current political governance of the country enforces the age old casteist and hierarchical social patterns for the sake of reinstating pseudo-nationalist heritages, the subaltern political philosophy of Ambedkar becomes more significant and valid. Today, in India, where dalits/adivasis, the tribals, and the unorganized sections of the country face various kinds of violence and violations, invocations for a social democracy is so crucial. Dalits and the religious minorities are being tortured in the name of their menial jobs, food culture and social position as it is imposed upon them on the basis of the caste phenomenology. Hindutva ideology with its political power assumes a new form of Empire in India today. Ambedkar's political philosophy of justice (Dhamma) becomes more significant today as it invokes the formation of the radical political community that stands for the weaker sections. Hindutva as a transcendent ideology legitimizes a sacred 'beyond' in order to substantiate the hierarchical ordering of the society. Dhamma offers a sharp critique of this transcendental legitimacy of the sacred and seeks radical political practices of justice to restructure the social imagination in favor of the weak and vulnerable, especially the dalits. What is interesting is that the present Hindutva government offers venerations of Ambedkar effigies while consciously suppressing any kind of the eruptions of his ideological manifestations.

Church in India which has had the heritage of challenging the sovereign power of the state become silent and mute due to its fear on the closure of their institutions like educational institutions and hospitals, their major income generating programs. Furthermore, as we have discussed earlier church in India is yet to develop a radical political theology of justice as it encounters the new nuances of the Empire. For that matter, Ambedkar's political philosophy of justice becomes a meaningful interlocutor to envisage a relevant postcolonial, anti-imperial, materialist, political theology in India today. Christian theology is invoked here to envisage a materialist turn, repudiating the sovereignty of the wholly other God and to take an immanent turn to become the "being thus" of the political practice of justice. Indian Christian theology including Dalit theology never engaged with this materialist notion of (no) God.[28]

Secondly, Ambedkar's political philosophy of religion invites Christian theology to have a postcolonial turn to de-colonize its Euro-centric dogmatics and doctrines. As Catherine Keller contends while delineating the potentiality of the postcolonial theologies in the contemporary context of Empire, "With its (Christian Theology's) imperial success the church, one might argue, absorbed an idolatry of identity: a metaphysical Babel of unity, an identity that homogenizes the multiplicities it absorbs, that either excludes or subordinates every creaturely other, alter, subaltern."[29] The challenge that the Ambedkar's philosophy of religion poses before Christian Theology is that it is to be rooted in the subaltern ethical and religious epistemologies embodied in their political practices of transformation: rather than the Euro-centric "imperio-colonial" epistemologies and doctrines that are impotent in resisting the Vedic-transcendental epistemologies and theologies. The challenge before Christian Theology in India is to reconfigure its epistemological and philosophical foundations that delimit its potential to become a subaltern political practice which locates its epistemological habitation in Indian materialistic philosophies and heterodox religious traditions.

Finally, Ambedkar's philosophy of religion invites Christian Theology to take a polydoxical turn. Polydoxy, as Catherine Keller and Laurel C. Schneider define, signifies the multiple origins of its resources such as doxa, opinion, heritage, and tradition.[30] As Edward Said once said, "the origin is always plural." Polydoxy as it celebrates multiplicity, manyness and pluralism, denies any kind of fundamentalism as we see in the case of Hindutva ideology. Unlike the orthodox tradition, Polydoxy celebrates inter-disciplinarity, trans-disciplinarity and even non-disciplinarity. It is to encounter, articulate, embody and contest the multiplicity of Indian religious traditions in favor of the weak and the agonized. As Richard Kearney opines, Polydoxy is the *anatheist* point where the so-called theists and atheists sit together, dream together, and do theology/ politics together for the disenfranchised.[31] For the church it is an invitation to validate the multiplicity of its being, becoming and belonging in this world of manyness. Religion in this polydoxical turn becomes 'religion without religion' and it is the moment when Christianity is provoked to be a kenotic Christianity (Christianity without religion: Dietrich Bonheoffer). In other words, the context of Empire is the polydoxic moment for the Christian church to deny the fixity of its dogmatics and the idolatry of its traditions and thereby de-imperialize itself.

End Notes

1 Ambedkar's major contention with Indian democracy was its inability to ensure justice for the excluded people especially dalits. According to Ambedkar, in a social system where people are excluded on the basis of their birth needs radical modification and revisions along with some special provisions for the excluded ones to ensure their participation the democratic processes. B. R. Ambedkar, *Annihilation of Caste* (New Delhi: Navayana, 2014).

2 Dewey was Ambedkar's teacher in the Columbia University, New York. There are some studies that define Ambedkar as a statist. It is a misunderstanding of Ambedkar's political thought and a misreading of the Deweyan pragmatism. Dewey had never been a statist. For e.g. Keith Hebden, *Dalit Theology and Christian Anarchism* (USA & London: Ashagate, 2011), 87.

3 Eleanor Zelliot, *Ambedkar's World: The Making of Babasaheb and the Dalit Movement* (New Delhi: Navayana, 2004), 76.

4 P. Sanal Mohan, "Religion, Social Space, and Identiy: The Prathyaksha Raksha Daiva Sabha and the Making of Cultural Boundaries in Twentieth Century Kerala," in *Journal of South Asian Studies*, n.s. XXXVIII (1), April, 2005.

5 Pradeep Gokhale, 'Dr. Ambedkar as a Philosopher: Beyond Reductionism,' in *The Philosophy of Dr. B. R. Amedkar*, edited by Pradeep Gokhale (Pune: Indian Philosophical Quarterly Publication, 2008), 1-25.

6 Anupama Rao, 'Revisiting interwar thought: Stigma, labor, and the immanence of caste-class,' in *The Political Philosophies of Antonio Gramsci and B. R. Ambedkar: Itineraries of Dalits and Subalterns* edited by Cosimo Zene (London & New York: Routledge, 2013), 43-58.

7 Ibid., 48-49.

8 Ibid., 52.

9 Ibid., 55.

10 Pradeep Gokhale, 'Dr. Ambedkar as a Philosopher: Beyond Reductionism,' 6.

11 Kancha Illaiah, *God as Political Philosopher, Buddha's Challenge to Brahmanism* (Calcutta: Samya, 2000).

12 Gail Omvedt, *Buddhism in India* (New Delhi: Sage Publications, 2003).

13 Raosaheb Kasbe, *Ambedkar and Marx* cited by Pradeep Gokhale, 'Dr. Ambedkar as a Philosopher: Beyond Reductionism, 13.

14 *Babasaheb Ambedkar: Writings and Speeches*, Vol. 3, (Bombay Education Department, Government of Maharashtra, 1989), 451.

15 Kesava Kumar, 'Political Philosophy of B. R. Ambedkar: A Critical Understanding, *International Research Journal of Social Sciences*, Vol. 1 No. 2, pp. 193-210, 2008, Pondicherry University, Pondicherry.

16 Ibid., 4-5.

17 Cf. Rev. Fr. J. Jans. S. J. *The Depressed Classes: A Chronological Documentation*, Vol. 1. (Ranchi: Catholic Press, 1935), 102-3.

18 Harish Wnkhede, 'The Political and Social in the Dalit Movement Today,' in *Economic & Political Weekly*, February 9, 2008, 50-57.

19 Valerian Roudrigues, ed., *The Essential Writings of B. R. Ambedkar* (New Delhi: Oxford University Press, 2002), 61.

20 Babasaheb Ambedkar: *Writings and Speeches*, edited by Vasant moon and Hari Narke, Vol. 17 (3): 503, Mumbai Education Department, Government of Maharashtra.

21 Jon Soske, 'The other prince, Ambedkar, constitutional democracy, and the agency of the law,' in *The Political Philosophies*, 70.

22 Douglas Harink, ed., *Paul, Philosophy and the Theopolitical Vision, Critical Engagements with Agamben, Badiou, Zizek, and Others* (Eugene: Cascade Books, 2010).

23 Akash Singh Rathore and Ajay Verma, eds., *B. R. Ambedkar: the Budha and his Dharma, A Critical Edition* (New Delhi: Oxford University Press, 2011), 221.

24 Giorgio Agamben, *The Coming Community*, trans., Michael Hardt (Minneapolis: University of Minnesota Press, 1993), 90.
25 *Babasaheb Ambedkar: Writings and Speeches*, Vol.7, (Bombay Education Department, Government of Maharashtra, 1989), 471-2.
26 James Massey, *Dr. B.R. Ambedkar: A Stud in Just Society*, New Delhi: Center for Dalit/ Subaltern Studies, 2003), 60; Eleanor Zelliot, *Ambedkar's World: The Making of Babasaheb and the Dalit Movement* (Delhi: Navayana, 2004), 143-168.
27 Ambedkar, cited from Dr. S. Lourdunathan, *Theology as Social: Relevance of Ambedkar in Theologizing in India: Search for an Authentic Way of Becoming the Word of God* (Bangalore: CISRS, 2016).
28 For a detailed discussion see, Y.T. Vinayaraj, *Dalit Theology after Continental Philosophy* (New York: Palgrave Macmillan, 2016).
29 Catherine Keller, "The Love of Postcolonialism: Theology in the Interstices of Empire," in *Postcolonial Theologies, Divinity and Empire*, edited by Catherine Keller, Michael Nausner and Mayra Rivera (Missouri: Chalice Press, 2004), 223.
30 Catherine Keller and Laurel C. Schneider, eds., *Polydoxy, Theology of Multiplicity and Relation* (London and New York: Routledge, 2011).
31 Anatheism is the world coined by Richard Kearney. For Richard Kearney Anatheism is a position in between theism and atheism and relativism and absolutism. See Richard Kearney, *Anatheism: Returning to God after God* (New York: Columbia University Press, 2010).

5

Theology as Political Practice
Political Theology after Gilles Deleuze

Introduction

Gilles Deleuze is one of the most influential and important French philosophers of the second half of the twentieth century who offered a materialist philosophy of life. Critiquing the modern western tradition of representation, Deleuze offered a political ontology of becoming that dismantled the dichotomy between thinking and living, transcendence and immanence, theory and practice, philosophy and politics, being and becoming. According to Claire Colebrook, Gilles Deleuze is a "practical philosopher" who exhorted us to think about our being as becoming in terms of our differences, multiplicities, and singularities.[1] The task of Deleuze was to deconstruct the unitarian subjectivity formations in the modern institutional structures and to offer a subjectivity of fluidity, liberation and freedom. For him, the western notion of subjectivity is transcendental in content and tied to a metaphysical logic which renders political life (daily life) as ephemeral, subordinate or invalid. On the contrary, Deleuze offered a political ontology of pure immanence which is not at all immanent to transcendence or any other representational axiomatics; but immanent to itself.[2]

This chapter deals with Deleuze's political philosophy of ontology and signifies it for a contemporary political practice of Christian theology. Since Deleuze signifies daily life as valid and significant, Christian theology in Deleuzian framework becomes a practical liberation theology. In fact, Deleuze's post-Marxian heritage provokes Christian theology to cross over even the Liberation theology in order to be immanentized and enmattered. However, connecting Deleuze with Christian theology is not easy since he is skeptical about the fecundity of theology to attend the immanent concerns of life. For Deleuze, Theology is always transcendental in content and practice and founded on dichotomies such as God-world, sacred-secular, and transcendence and immanence.[3] However, there are political theologians who explore the possibility of connecting Deleuze with theology in order to reconstruct a new materialist theology on 'the weight of the world' (Mark Lewis Taylor). Taking the cue from them, this chapter tries to explore the connectivity between Deleuze and theology on the matrix of 'Life' for reconstructing a radical political theology today.[4]

Gilles Deleuze: Life Sketch and Works

Gilles Deleuze was born on 18th January 1925 in Paris. Deleuze's father was an engineer who had also served in World War I. When Germans began their occupation in France in June 1940, his family had to move to Normandy where Deleuze spent one year for schooling. One of the events that influenced his early life was when Deleuze's elder brother, who was involved in German resistance during German occupation of France, was arrested by the Nazis for resistance activities. He was deported but he died on the train to Auschwitz.[5] Deleuze studied the history of philosophy at the Sorbonne. After his studies, he held various teaching positions at Paris and the provinces from 1953-1969. He was married to Fanny (Denise Paul) Grandjouan, a French translator of D. H. Lawrence and raised two children with her.

Deleuze's work reveals his philosophical inclinations within the history of philosophy in the West. He published his first book in 1953 with the title *Empiricism and Subjectivity* which reveals his leaning towards David Hume. He continued his writings: *Nietzsche and Philosophy* (1962); *Kant's Critical Philosophy* (1963); *Proust and Signs* (1964); *Bergsonism* (1966); *Difference and Repetition* (1968); *Spinoza and the Problem of Expression* (1968); and *Logic of Sense* (1969). In 1969 he found a permanent teaching position at the University of Paris VIII in Vincennes where he gave weekly seminars. In collaboration with Felix Guattari, a radical psychoanalyst and political militant, Deleuze wrote *Anti Oedipus* (1972), *Kafka: Toward a Minor Literature* (1975), and *A Thousand Plateaus* (1980). In 1980's was a decade of independent work for Deleuze: *Francis Bacon: Logic of Sensation* (1981); *Cinema I: The Movement-Image* (1983); *Cinema II: The Time-Image* (1985); *Foucault* (1986); and *The Fold: Leibniz and the Baroque* (1988). Along with Guattari, Deleuze published *What is Philosophy?* in 1991.[6] Despite his acute ill health, he did manage to publish a remarkable short essay "Immanence: A Life" in 1995, before taking his own life on November 4, 1995.

His intention to write a series of works on the figures in the history of western philosophy such as David Hume, Henri Bergson, Nietzsche, Kant and Spinoza was to unearth the politics of the western philosophy of ontology. According to Deleuze, the western philosophy was constituted by the "identitarian" traditions that overlooked the notion of difference. Taking a new turn from the "transcendental" tradition of the west that rendered identity as unitarian, Deleuze, on the other hand, qualified subject formation as "differential," "immanent," and "singular." By critiquing the Kantian-Hegelian transcendentalism, Deleuze follows Spinoza, Leibniz, Hume, Nietzsche and Bergson to formulate the materialist ideas of virtuality and multiplicity in the process of the subject formation.

Deleuze takes his 'philosophy of difference' from Spinoza who spoke about the univocity in ontology. This univocity is not unitarian, identitarian, and dialectical; but it is differentiating within itself in terms of multiplicities and singularities. It is this idea of univocity in ontology that leads him to the philosophy of being as "becoming." For Deleuze, being as becoming is an internally differentiating mechanism that leads the society to 'assemblages.' Assemblages are the connections of bodies as 'desiring machines.'[7] According to Deleuze, the world is no longer a continuous world defined by its pre-established harmony; instead, it is composed of divergences, bifurcations, and incompossibilities—a chaotic universe—"chaosmos" as he calls it. This idea is well-explained in his masterpiece *Difference and Repetition* (1968). Commenting on this book, Michael Foucault once said: "One day, perhaps, this century will be called Deleuzian."[8]

Methodologically speaking Deleuze is a Spinozist and Nietzschean and thus he finds his location in the poststructuralist philosophical school of thought. At the same time, his inclination to psychoanalysis through Guattari takes him to the tradition of Jacques Lacan and Judith Butler. Since he is a product of the 1968 May Revolution in France, he becomes a close associative of Michael Foucault whose works on power and knowledge influence Deleuze substantially to formulate a contemporary political ontology. Deleuze is basically a Marxian; through Marx only he comes to the idea of the materiality of the everyday consciousness. Alluding to Marx, Deleuze argues that it is the human material activity that contributes to the existence of specific arrangements of thought and matter.[9] Here, Deleuze overcomes the dichotomy between subject-object, thought-matter, and theory-practice. He offers studies on the affects/effects of neo-capitalism and micro-fascism upon human bodies and human subjectivities through his work *Capitalism and Schizophrenia* (1977). Deleuze proposes a political programme that attempts to transform subjectivity, society and ecology through collective experimentation with production and desire. This is the task accomplished in *A Thousand Plateaus: Capitalism and Schizophrenia* (1987).

The works of Deleuze have been applied in cultural and aesthetic criticism, especially film and literature. Due to its concern with materialism and the mechanics of the production of representation, the Deleuzian thoughts are applied in the study of information. Deleuzian ideas of singularities and becomings are appropriated by feminists to understand and analyze the subjective formation of women in our society. The People like Manuel DeLanda, on the other hand, look into the theory of assemblages in order to provide a creative discussion on the political philosophy of society. The most contemporary work that received much attention of the global academic community is the trilogy of Michael Hardt and Antonio Negri—*Empire, Multitude* and *Commonwealth*—through which they offer a materialist analysis of the neo-liberal economy and culture and advocating resistance by the 'multitude'—the political ontology of the dispossessed in the era of globalization. In a nut shell, Deleuzian thought world is as wide as it covers philosophy, literature, art, culture, psychology and politics. However, if any one wants to focus on the cardinal point that Deleuze wishes to pose, it is nothing but the philosophy of Life—the power of human to become more than human and the world to the world that is not yet revealed.[10]

Major Philosophical Concepts of Deleuze

For Deleuze, philosophy creates concepts. Concepts are not labels or names that we attach to things; they produce an orientation or a direction for thinking. Deleuze believes that concepts create 'new connections for thinking, opening up whole new 'planes of thought.'[11] According to Deleuze, concepts provide expanding and overlapping connections. For Deleuze, concepts are interconnected and overlapped each other and thereby offer us a detailed study on the political ontology of Life. Thus understanding Deleuzian concepts is a prerequisite for understanding Deleuze and his philosophy of political ontology. This section deals with some of his important concepts through which he elaborates his political philosophy of ontology.

1. Desire

It was Karl Marx who taught us to define philosophy as the practice of life. According to Marx thinking is not the passive representation of the world; rather it allows new events and possibilities and thereby creates a new world. It is in the thinking process that we create and transform our world through political and social existence and thus Marx held that theory is practical and political. Engaging with Marx, Michel Foucault highlighted the question of power that constitutes our subjectivities and social relations. Unlike Marx, power in Foucault is positive in which we are able to reconstitute ourselves and transform our social relations. For Foucault, power is the very force of life that reorients, recreates and transforms ourselves and our social relations. Locating himself in this tradition, Gilles Deleuze presented the concept of 'desire' as the creative and productive power of immanent life. For Deleuze, life as desire has no single foundation or ground that ought to be obeyed or something it wants or lacks (Freud); rather 'it is just a productive and creative energy, a desire of flux, force and difference.' It is a revolutionary desire 'that we need to *think* in ways that will disrupt our common sense and everyday life.'[12]

2. Representation

Deleuze challenged the dominant belief that we know and experience our world through imposed structures of representation. Instead, he brings in the idea of desire—the power of creative thinking that takes us out of our fixed dogmas of common sense and into entirely new ways of experiencing the world. For him, there are no essential meanings to the substances or an art; but it is the potential of the desire or the power of the thinking that produce artistic events or events of art. Here, Deleuze connects philosophy with other essential powers of thinking such as science and art. Deleuze argues that all our values are representations and constructions. They are tied to some transcendental essences and ultimate epistemological foundations. Interrogating those ultimate foundations, Deleuze asks us to think about their functions not just their ultimate meanings. When we look at a text our intention should be on how it works rather than what it means. Art, for Deleuze, is not just a set of representations; but it is through art that we can see the connections and the styles of thinking. Art can show the force or productive power of our values.[13] Thus meanings are immanent; not transcendental.

3. Difference

Following Nietzsche, Deleuze interrogates the unitarian thinking of the West, as it was offered by modernity, especially the

Hegelian dialectics. According to Hegelian dialectics, the reality is generated through the antagonistic construction of polar opposite phenomena—via negativity. Deleuze sees it as a theological outlook where differences are always subsumed to an underlying unity; contradictions always seek a higher synthesis. For Deleuze, this unitarian (dialectical) ideology, undermines the 'subterranean differential mechanisms' that constitute reality through the will to power. Here dialectics remains, as Deleuze explains, "a perpetual misinterpretation of difference itself, a confused inversion of genealogy." On the contrary, difference, for him, is not a product of negativity; rather, it is "a notion of desire which is productive and creative. Difference is positive as it allows us to feel the connectivity; rather than dichotomy. Life is deferential. Every living being exists in a state of constant becoming of differentiation. Each event of life differentiates itself differentially. There are linguistic differences, genetic differences, sensible differences, chemical differences, animal differences and imperceptible differences. As Claire Colebrook explains "Life itself is difference, and this difference is in each case different."[14] The whole task of Deleuze is to affirm our irreducible singularities over against the totalizing ideologies and ontologies like modernity, fascism and capitalism.

4. Immanence

According to Deleuze, the key error of western thought has been transcendence. It was Immanuel Kant (1724-1804) and Edmund Husserl (1854-1938) who established the philosophy of transcendence in western tradition over against immanence. Here, transcendence is conceived as the outside of our consciousness or experience. We experience the real world as transcendent or as external. In this view, there can be a real world 'outside me.' The problem with this thinking is that it locates the legitimizing point outside life such as God, morality and identity. The western notion of transcendence renders immanence as its binary opposite. Here, transcendence and immanence are not just dualities; rather they are ordered in a hierarchical pattern. Transcendence is higher than immanence. Immanence has no intrinsic value in it. It is always dependent on transcendence. In contradiction to this idea of dependent transcendence, Deleuze argues for the immanence of life which has no outside and nothing other than itself. For him, life is immanent in itself as the power of creation. The power of creation does not lie outside the world like God—the legitimizing point; life itself is a process of creative power.[15] Thinking is not an act of representation of the world; rather it is a part of the flux of the world. For Deleuze, to think is not to represent life but to transform and act upon it.

5. Multiplicity

Multiplicity, in Deleuzian understanding, is a collection of parts. It is not just differences; but differentiations. The parts are connected with each other to form a machine—assemblage—a kind of social connectivity of beings. Deleuze makes a distinction between extensive and intensive multiplicity. Extensive multiplicity is a multiplicity of some distinct, generalized and bounded body. A family tree where all members are connected with each other is an example for extensive multiplicity. A multiplicity of this kind is always a multiplicity of a distinct, generalized and bounded body. Unlike this, an intensive multiplicity is not a multiplicity of a bounded body or an identifiable measure; rather, it is a substantive multiplicity through bodies which are bound to a genetic mutation within it that crosses even the bodies and alter them to a third. It is a kind of connectedness based on the differences rather than similarities and thus envisages dynamism of becoming. It is a becoming multiple.[16] This means that life does not unfold itself in One single form or manner; there are multiplicities of folds and flows. Multiplicities are the "expressions" of the immanent life.

6. Rhizome

Deleuze and Guattari develop the philosophical concept of rhizome as a fluid model of thinking based on the botanical development of a mass of roots. As a botanical rhizome (or root mass) extends and expands in subterranean, underground, spaces unpredictably without any fixed pattern, concepts, creations, and interpretations shift and develop in an organic progression of ideas. The rhizome as a model of thought embraces multiplicities and rejects the notion of clear beginning, middle and end. The rhizome does not follow pre-determined paths or seek a specific destination. It is unpredictable. Rhizome signifies an image of thought that can freely reflect the changeable character of creativity, self-expression and identity and cultural endeavour. Deleuze and Guattari define it clearly: "the rhizome pertains to a map that must be produced, constructed, a map that is always detachable, connectible, reversible, modifiable and has multiple entryways and exists and its own lines of flight."[17] In contrast to the hierarchical, dichotomous, unitarian identity thinking, rhizome offers a thinking pattern of connectivity, multiplicity, fluidity and relationality. As Steven Best and Douglas Kellner contend, rhizomes are non-hierarchical systems of deterritorialized lines that connect with other lines in random, unregulated relationships.[18] For Deleuze, "Nature is a rhizome, where roots are taproots with a more multiple, lateral, and circular system of ramification, rather than a dichotomous one."[19]

Towards a Theology of Immanence

'Immanence' is an important hallmark of Deleuze's philosophy. Deleuze, through his philosophy of immanence destabilizes the established foundations of western thought whether it is philosophy or theology. Christian Theology, as it emerges as a product of western thought, is transcendental in content and practice. Destabilizing the transcendental foundation of the western thought demands the total reconfiguration of the epistemological foundation of theology. That is why Deleuze once said 'dealing with immanence is to embrace a dangerous idea, one that engulfs sages and gods.'[20] Transcendence, for Deleuze, is an illusionary concept that theology tries to legitimize the foundation of all knowledges. Deleuze criticizes transcendence for subjecting Life to the logic of identity and sameness. Deleuze affirms that whether it is theology or politics, transcendence legitimizes the sovereign, hierarchical, dichotomous political system and immanent life as a subordinate to it. The problem of transcendence is that it denies the affirmation of difference in itself. It accommodates even the opposite as an exteriority. It subordinates everything. The political correlate of transcendence is sovereign: the absolute political power. This is the critical point of departure for Deleuze to configure a political philosophy of immanence as it provides creative potential for freedom and transformation. Thus he insists, 'hunt down transcendence' wherever it is found in order for immanence to be realized.'[21]

In contradiction to the transcendental thinking of the west, Deleuze offers a philosophy of 'pure immanence' which is immanent to itself. Deleuze argues that transcendence is just an illusion and 'there is only immanent Life, there cannot be anything exterior to this life.'[22] For him, immanence is not simply an idea or a concept, but as the pre-philosophical horizon against which thinking can be creative and productive. This pre-philosophical character of this horizon is called 'pure immanence.' For Deleuze, immanence is not a technical philosophical concept; but it is a matter how one lives his or her life. Immanence is the only reality of life. Transcendence is only a temporary phenomenon or effect taking place purely within the plane of immanence. Transcendence is constituted within the plane of immanence only. However, for Deleuze, the immanent has two sides, a virtual and an actual one; the virtual is as real as the actual. The virtual saves the actual from representation and identification. Here, the virtual may assume the status of the transcendent; but Deleuze argues that both actual and virtual function within the plane of pure immanence in order to create intensities of becomings. The virtual is the plane of immanence on which processes of actualization take place.[23]

Deleuze brings in the idea of univocity to challenge the bi-vocity of the western thought. Over against the transcendental thinking of the western philosophy/theology which legitimizes a dual thinking (e.g. God and His creation) within the logic of the 'Oneness,' Deleuze, argues for univocity which happens in the plane of immanence. However, this univocity doesn't efface or render subordinate the differences in between. Alluding to Nietzsche, Deleuzian univocity is inextricably linked to creativity, to the infinite productiveness of being that affirms difference. Deleuze explains this differentiated understanding of being:

The univocity of Being does not mean that there is one and the same Being; on the contrary, beings are multiple and different, they are always produced by a disjunctive synthesis, and they themselves are disjoined and divergent, *membra disjecta*. The univocity of Being signifies that Being is Voice that it is said, and that it is said in one and the same 'sense' of everything about which it is said. That of which it is said is not at all the same, but Being is the same for everything about which it is said.[24]

How does Deleuze define difference in his idea of univocity? In Deleuze, difference is thought internally, within both being and beings, as differentiation of being. This notion of 'internal difference' is taken from Bergson who created this idea to avoid the negativity of the western tradition. In western tradition, as Hegel appropriates, difference is exteriority. Through this idea of 'internal difference,' Deleuze aims to unite 'the One' and 'the Many' –the established dichotomies of the western tradition. For Deleuze, being is difference. Thus, univocity does not equal identity, and all beings are seen to be what they are: not the same.[25] In this idea of univocity everything is in the same plane of immanence and nothing is located in a hierarchical order. This idea of univocity is highly problematical for theology since it is founded on the idea of equivocity between God and His creation (Augustine and Thomas Aquinas). In the idea of Deleuzian univocity, there is no hierarchical relationship between God and creation; but they are in a same plane of immanence. According to Deleuze, God and creatures share an identity of form, 'while permitting no confusion of essence.' Here, Deleuze affirms the irreducible singularities of both as it is the same in the case of all creatures.

The idea of the plane of immanence makes philosophy and theology practical. The fundamental aspect of thinking, for Deleuze, is life. Alluding to Spinoza, Deleuze defines life as the way of being. In order to make clear his idea of life in terms of anti-anthropomorphism, he calls it *impersonal* life. Life is impersonal in the sense, it is like a field of energy in which the smallest particles are constantly moving, colliding with each other, and forming molecules that dissolve again after a while. Even these smallest particles, as quantum physics has taught, are not really stable particles but pure waves of energy. Thus the Deleuzian plane of immanence is ever creative, productive and of course, becoming in itself.

However, the immanentization of transcendence is not a new quest in the Christian theology. The contemporary liberation theologians, feminist theologians, ecotheologies, eco-feminist theologies and postcolonial theologies have initiated different kinds of initiatives. Then, what is special in Deleuzian pure immanence? All these Immanentist theologies wanted to create a new 'sensitivity to the horizontal sacred.'[26] The ecotheologies try to restore the relationship between human beings and the rest of creation. They want to reinstate the ethical connectivity between humanity and the nature. This implies a non-hierarchical, immanent view of creation. Sallie McFague's study on creation as the 'body of God' is one of the best examples of that counter-transcendent tradition. However, alluding to Deleuze, Luke Higgins argues that it is nothing but a Neo-Platonist tendency to provide an immanent flavor to the originally transcendent God. Luke Higgins makes it clear:

Multiplicity and diversity are affirmed but only insofar as they can be traced back or added up to a higher, 'macrotranscendent' unity. If the divine continues to function as the guiding logic, or telos, for all that lies beneath or within it, does not the singularity of the transcendent divine consistently end up trumping the multiplicity of an immanent divine?[27]

Luke Higgins argues that even in these counter-transcendent traditions we see the glimpses of a transcendent God may be in the form of 'macrotranscendent' spirit. The feminist theologians like Rosemary Radford Ruether who envisions a God of 'immanent transcendence' provides a space for a 'macrotranscendent God' in the form of "Gaia'—the internal spirit that takes life towards the *telos*. Deleuzian pure immanence neither provides any space for such a God or spirit, nor legitimizes any pre-conceived eschaton. Therefore, Luke Higgins suggests:

Instead of seeking the divine on the level of what we have called the macrotranscendent, what if we turn our gaze toward the smallest, most dynamic microelements of reality imaginable? What if we envision the divine not as an infinite singularity but an infinitesimal multiplicity? The divine, then would no longer function to validate from on high a single structure or pattern of ecological relationships.[28]

As Bruno Latour contends, the order of this world is not pre-given but this 'micro-god' animates all creative becomings in the universe. It is this micro-god—a God of process is the potential of the infinite dynamic of the earth. In Deleuze, the plane of immanence is the divine matrix for the ecological interconnectedness. This God of immanence is the God who lives with us, that gives us life and that we must enable to let live. Kristien Justaert argues that "Humanity has to make the leap beyond itself to form a new community with the earth, and this requires hope and belief, a belief in god as an immanent microprocess."[29] Deleuze offers a new immanent ecotheology: "it is possible that the problem now concerns the one who believes in the world, and not even in the existence of the world but in its possibilities of movements and intensities, so as once again to give birth to new existence, closer to animals and rocks."[30] Signifying Deleuzian pure immanence for ecotheology, Rijin M. George explores the possibility of constructing the creator God as multiplicity in Indian context.[31]

Deleuze as a Political Theologian

The whole project of Deleuze is to liberate human beings from the mechanisms of oppression. The notion of transcendence or representation locates liberation in some axiomatic outside. For Deleuze, the becoming ethical is political. For him, political is not ideological; but ontological in content and practice. The desire is a potential force in the being that leads bodies into multiplicities and thus become political. Desire is a social force which is not bound to the individual. Deleuze and Guattari in *Anti-Oedipus* and *A Thousand Plateaus* argue that in the contemporary society, our desire is captivated in the axiomatic of capitalism.[32] According to them, capitalism deterritorializes our desires by freeing it from the old axiomatic and creating new flows of decoding. They explain how capitalism captivates our desires through decoding: "While decoding doubtless means understanding and translating a code, it also means destroying the code as such, assigning it an archaic, folkloric or residual function."[33] It is a kind of deterritorialization into our practices based on the previous forms of social organization.

Capitalism, instead, offers a new axiomatic—the rules of ordering the society—changing the society into a profit oriented society. According to Deleuze, capitalism is a form of anti-production which produces only the flow of money not the materialist production. The role of state in this capitalist paradigm is to moderate the flow of the deterritorialization of capital. Deleuze, along with Guattari argue that 'the state pervades all production and becomes coextensive with capitalism.'[34] The state becomes just a correlative mechanism to the abstract flow of capital. This free flow of capital entails a decentering subject, which become schizophrenic—a post humanist subjectivity. However, for Deleuze and Guattari, the formation of the post humanist subjectivity—schizophrenic can be the potential site for the formation assemblages—the social collectivity based on multiplicities and singularities and thereby resists the deterritorialization of capitalist desires. They call it 'micropolitics.'[35] Micropolitics is the constructive political action that comes forth from the margins of capitalism. It is a collective political program of becoming the margin—the minority. Thus, they call micropolitics as the minority politics.[36]

Engaging with this Deleuzian idea of 'becoming minority' (assemblage), Kristien Justaert offers a radical ecclesiology in the context of neo-capitalism:

It [Assemblage] is a wholly contingent conjunction of bodies (human and non-human alike), a collection of dissimilar that coincide but also share a 'belief in this world.' In relation to the theological appreciation of this Deleuzian concept, it can already be noted that this kind of community will have large repercussions on the concept of Christian identity because it is precisely not a shared identity that brings different components of an assemblage together or binds them together.[37]

As Justaert contents, church as the assemblage demands a doctrinal re-configuration of Christianity. In Deleuzian framework, Christian theology of God needs to be de-transcendentalized. The Christian community needs to be restructured in the form of a non-hierarchical community. It is expected to be a community of becoming—becoming minority. Church as a becoming minority practices micropolitics through which it challenges the all kinds of representative mechanisms like fascism and capitalism. Church as an assemblage embodies hope within it not as a telos but as a political ontology of becoming. God of this church takes the form of life in its pure immanence as we see in the life of Jesus Christ. Slavoj Zizek completes what Deleuze wanted to say about the pure-immanent God in Jesus: "What the incarnation teaches is not only that God becomes human; but also that God becomes in and of the world, and thereby, theology is rendered not simply anthropological (Feuerbach), but political."[38]

Conclusion

Deleuze as the philosopher of pure immanence dismantles the transcendental, representational, and the axiomatic foundations that render the immanent, material, and earthly life as subordinate, dependent, and invalid-other. Life in its fullness is materialistic in content and political in practice. The world, human and non-human which constitutes Life is totally free from its axiomatic foundations and metaphysical foundations. These axiomatic representations legitimize dichotomy, hierarchy and disparity. The desire is nothing but a creative and productive power that connects human beings internally and materially with the other forms of life. Desire that creates rhizomatic connections enable society to form a collective subjectivity which is multiple, fluid, and differentiated within it. Society as assemblage exercises its collective force to counter the overarching systems and structures like fascism and capitalism. It is a life of multiplicity and singularity. It initiates micropolitics though which human beings experience the *telos* not as a distant hope; but as hope here and now. Deleuze invites, invokes, and interrogates Christian theology to be immanentized and to be political in content and practice. In Deleuzian understanding, church can be envisaged as a political ontology of difference that practices micropolitics in the contemporary context of fascism and corporate capitalism.

End Notes

1 Claire Colebrook, *Understanding Deleuze* (Australia: Allen & Unwin, 2002), xii.

2 Ibid., 51.

3 Kristien Justaert, *Theology after Deleuze* (London & New York: Continuum, 2012), 5.

4 The capital letter 'L' denotes life as the ecology of relations.

5 *Stanford Encyclopedia of Philosophy*, "Gilles Deleuze," https://plato.stanford.edu/entries/deleuze.

6 Guattari was a trained Lacanian psychoanalyst. He has been politically active from an early age, and participated in the events of May 1968. He has collaborated with Italian theorist Antonio Negri and has been involved in the 'autonomy' movement which seeks an independent revolutionary movement outside of the structures of organized parties. Deleuze and Guattari follow the general tenor of Foucault's critique of modernity. Like Foucault, their central concern is with modernity as an unparalleled historical stage of domination based on the proliferation of normalizing discourses and institutions that pervade all aspects of social existence and everyday life. For more details see, Steven Best and Douglas Kellner, *Postmodern Theory: Critical Interrogations* (New York: The Guildford Press, 1991), 76-110.

7 Manuel DeLanda, *A New Philosophy of Society: Assemblage Theory and Social Complexity* (London & New York: Bloomsbury, 2006), 3.

8 Michael Foucault, "Theatrum Philosophicum", *Critique* 282: 885.

9 Philip Goodchild, "Gilles Deleuze (1925-95) and Felix Guattari (1930-9)," in *Contemporary Critical Theorists: From Lacan to Said,* edited by Jon Simons (UK: Edinburgh University Press, 2004), 170-171.

10 Claire Colebrook, *Deleuze* (London & New York: Routledge, 2002), 25.

11 Ibid., 15.

12 Claire Colebrook, *Understanding Deleuze,* xv.

13 Ibid., xxxii.

14 Patrice Haynes, *Immanent Transcendence: Reconfiguring Materialism in Continental Philosophy* (London & New York: Bloomsbury, 2012), 27.

15 Claire Colebrook, *Understanding Deleuze,* xxxiii.

16 Ibid., xxvi.

17 Gilles Deleuze and Guattari, *A Thousand Plateaus: Capitalism and Schizophrenia,* trans. R. Hurley, M Seem and H. R. Lane, Minneapolis: University Minnesota Press, 1987), 21.

18 Steven Best and Douglas Kellner, *Postmodern Theory: Critical Interrogations,* 102.

19 Gilles Deleuze and Guattari, *A Thousand Plateaus,* 8.

20 Gilles Deleuze and Guattari, *What is Philosophy?* trans. H. Tomlinson & G. Burchell (New York: Columbia University Press, 1994), 45.

21 Ibid., 48.

22 Ibid., 45.
23 Kristien Justaert, *Theology after Deleuze,* 14.
24 Gilles Deleuze, *The Logic of Sense,* trans. M Lester (New York: Columbia University Press, 1990), 179.
25 Kristien Justaert, *Theology after Deleuze,* 19.
26 Ibid., 34.
27 Luke Higgins, "Toward a Deleuze-Guattarian micropneumatologyof spirit-dust," 53 cited from Kristien Justaert, *Theology after Deleuze,* 35.
28 Luke Higgins cited from Kristien Justaert, *Theology after Deleuze,* 36.
29 Kristien Justaert, *Theology after Deleuze,* 37.
30 Gilles Deleuze and Guattari, *What is Philosophy?,* 55.
31 Rijin M. George, "Signifying Deleuze for a radical ecotheology in India," *unpublished BD thesis,* 2020, Mar Thoma Theological seminary, Kottayam.
32 Gilles Deleuze and Guattari, *A Thousand Plateaus,* 454; *Anti-Oedipus: Capitalism and Schizophrenia,* trans. R. Hurley, M Seem and H. R. Lane, Minneapolis: University Minnesota Press, 1987).
33 Gilles Deleuze and Guattari, *Anti-Oedipus,* 266.
34 Gilles Deleuze and Guattari, *A Thousand Plateaus,* 5001.
35 Ibid., 322.
36 Ibid., 323.
37 Kristien Justaert, *Theology after Deleuze,* 130.
38 Slavoj Zizek and John Milbank, *The Monstrosity of Christ: Paradox or Dialectic?,* ed. Creston Davis (Cambridge: MIT Press, 2009), 33.

Bibliography

Agamben, Giorgio. *The Coming Community.* Minneapolis: University of Minnesota Press, 1993.

________. *Potentialities: Collected Essays in Philosophy.* Trans. Daniel Heller-Roazen. Stanford: Stanford University Press, 1998.

________. *Homo Sacer: Sovereign Power and Bare Life.* Trans. Daniel Heller-Roazen. Stanford: Stanford University Press, 1998.

________. *Means Without End: Notes on Politics. Trans by Vincenzo Binetti and Cesare Casarino.* Minneapolis & London: University of Minnesota, 2000.

________. *The Time That Remains: A Commentary on the Letter to the Romans.* Trans. Patricia Dailey. Stanford, CA: Stanford University Press, 2005.

________. *State of Exception.* Chicago: The University of Chicago Press, 2005.

________. *The Kingdom and Glory: For a Theological Genealogy of Economy and Government.* Stanford: Stanford University Press, 2011.

________. *The Church and the Kingdom.* London, New York, Calcutta: Seagull Books, 2012.

________. *Opus Dei: An Archeology.* Trans. Adam Kotsko. Stanford, CA: Stanford University Press, 2013.

________. *The Highest Poverty: Monastic Rules and Form of Life.* Trans. Adam Kotsko. Stanford, CA: Stanford University Press, 2013.

Ambedkar. *Writings and Speeches.* Vol. 3, Bombay Education Department, Government of Maharashtra, 1989.

________. *Writings and Speeches.* Ed. Vasant moon and Hari Narke, Vol. 17 (3): 503, Mumbai Education Department, Government of Maharashtra.

________. *Annihilation of Caste* (New Delhi: Navayana, 2014).

Aschroft Bill, Grifith Gareth, and Helen Tiffin, eds. *Key Concepts in Post-colonial Studies.* London: Routledge, 1999.

Assmann, Jan. *Authority and Salvation: Political Theology in the Ancient Egypt, Israel, and Egypt.* Munich: Carl Hanser, 2000.

Badiou, Alain. *Saint Paul: The Foundation of Universalism.* Trans. Ray Brassier. Stanford: Stanford University Press, 2003.

Bennett, Jane. *Vibrant Matter: A Political Ecology of Things.* Durham and London: Duke University Press, 2010.

Best Steven and Kellner, Douglas. *Postmodern Theory: Critical Interrogations.* New York: The Guildford Press, 1991.

Bhabha, Homi. *The Location of Culture.* London & New York: Routledge, 1994.

Blanton, Ward & Vries, Hent De, eds. *Paul and the Philosophers.* New York: Fordham University Press, 2013.

Blanton Ward, Crockett Clayton, Robbins, Jeffrey W. and Vahanian, Noelle. *An Insurrectionist Manifesto: Four New Gospels for a Radical Politics.* New York: Columbia University Press, 2016.

Buchanan, Ian and Parr, Adrian, eds. *Deleuze and the Contemporary World.* Edinburgh: Edinburgh University Press, 2006.

Butler, Judith. *Parting Ways, Jewishness and Critique of Zionism.* New York: Columbia University Press, 2012.

Calarco M. and Steven Decaroli S., eds. *Giorgio Agamben: Sovereignty and Life.* Stanford, CA: Stanford University Press, 2007.

Caputo, John D. and Scanlon, Michel J., eds. *Transcendence and Beyond: A Postmodern Inquiry.* Bloomington and Indianapolis: Indiana University Press, 2007.

Chakrabarti, Simit. *The Impact of the Postcolonial Theories of Edward Said, Gayatri Spivak, and Homi Bhabha on Western Thought.* Lewiston: The Edwin Mellen Press, 2010.

Chaturvedi, Vinayak., ed. *Mapping Subaltern Studies and The Postcolonial.* London and New York: Verso, 2000.

Colebrook, Claire. *Gilles Deleuze.* New York and London: Routledge, 2001.

________. *Understanding Deleuze.* Australia: Allen & Unwin, 2002.

Coleman Rebecca and Ringrose Jessica, eds. *Deleuze and Research Methodologies.* Edinburgh: Edinburgh University Press, 2013.

Clemens J, Heron N and Murray A., eds. *The Work of Giorgio Agamben: Law, Literature, Life.* Edinburgh: Edinburgh University Press, 2008.

Crockett, Clayton, ed. *Religion and Violence in a Secular World: Toward a New Political Theology.* Charlottesville: University of Virginia Press, 2006.

________. *Radical Political Theology: Religion and Politics after Liberalism.* New York: Columbia University Press, 2011.

________. *Derrida after the End of Writing: Political Theology and New Materialism.* USA: Fordham University Press, 2018.

Crocket, Clayton and Robbins, Jeffrey W. *Religion, Politics, and the Earth: The New Materialism.* New York: Palgrave Macmillan, 2012.

DeLanda, Manuel. *A New Philosophy of Society: Assemblage Theory and Social Complexity.* London & New York: Bloomsbury, 2006.

Deleuze, Gilles. *The Logic of Sense.* Trans. M. Lester (New York: Columbia University Press, 1990.

________. *Difference & Repetition.* Trans. Paul Patton. New York: Columbia University Press, 1994.

Deleuze G. and Guattari. *A Thousand Plateaus: Capitalism and Schizophrenia.* Trans. R. Hurley, M. Seem and H. R. Lane. Minneapolis: University Minnesota Press, 1987.

________. *Anti-Oedipus: Capitalism and Schizophreni.,* Trans. R. Hurley, M. Seem and H. R. Lane. Minneapolis: University Minnesota Press, 1987.

________. *What is Philosophy?* Trans. H. Tomlinson & G. Burchell. New York: Columbia University Press, 1994.

Derrida. *The Gift of Death.* Trans. David Willis. Chicago: University of Chicago Press, 1995.

________. *Rogues: Two Essays on Reason.* Trans. Pascale-Anne Brault and Michael Naas. Stanford: Stanford University Press, 2005.

Edkins Jenny and Vaughan-Williams Nick. *Critical Theorists and International Relations.* London and New York: Routledge, 2009.

Eleanor Zelliot, Eleanor. *Ambedkar's World: The Making of Babasaheb and the Dalit Movement.* New Delhi: Navayana, 2004.

Fiorenza, Schussler F, Tanner K. and Welker M., eds., *Political Theology: Contemporary Challenges and Future Directions.* Louisville, CY: Westminster John Knox Press, 2013.

George P. G. and Vinayaraj Y. T., eds. *Reclaiming Manyness: Re-reading M. M. Thomas in the Light of Indiàn Christian Theologies.* Kolkata: SATHRI, 2015.

Gilbert—Moore. *Postcolonial Theory: Contexts, Practices and Politics.* London: Verso, 1997.

Gnanadasan, Aruna, ed. *Future of the Church in India.* Nagpur: NCCI, 1990.

Guru, Gopal and Sarukkai, Sunder. *The Cracked Mirror: An Indian Debate on Experience and Theory.* New Delhi: Oxford University Press, 2012.

Gutierrez, Gustavo. *A Theology of Liberation.* Maryknoll, NY: Orbis Books, 1973.

Gokhale, Pradeep, ed. *The Philosophy of Dr. B. R. Amedkar.* Pune: Indian Philosophical Quarterly Publication, 2008.

Hardt M. and Negri A. *Empire.* Cambridge, MA & London: Harvard University Press, 2000.

________. *The Multitude: War and Democracy in an Age of Empire.* New York: Penguin Press, 2004.

________. *Commonwealth.* Cambridge, MA: Harvard University Press, 2009.

Harink, Douglas, ed. *Paul, Philosophy and the Theopolitical Vision, Critical Engagements with Agamben, Badiou, Zizek, and Others.* Eugene: Cascade Books, 2010.

Haynes, Patrice. *Immanent Transcendence: Reconfiguring Materialism in Continental Philosophy.* London & New York: Bloomsbury, 2012.

Hernandez, Adriana. *Pedagogy, Democracy, and Feminism: Rethinking the Public Sphere.* New York: State University of New York Press, 1997.

Hovey, Craig and Philips, Elizabeth, eds. *Cambridge Companion to Christian Political Theology.* New York: Cambridge University Press, 2015.

Illaiah, Kancha. *God as Political Philosopher, Buddha's Challenge to Brahmanism.* Calcutta: Samya, 2000.

Jennings, Theodore W. Jennings Jr. *The Insurrection of the Crucified: The "Gospel of Mark" as Theological Manifesto.* Chicago, IL: exploration Press, 2003.

Justaert, Kristien. *Theology After Deleuze.* London and New York: Continuum, 2012.

Kathleen Ray, Darby, ed. *Theology that Matters: Ecology, Economy and God.* Minneapolis: Fortress Press, 2006.

Kearney, Richard. *Anatheism: Returning to God after God.* New York: Columbia University Press, 2010.

Kee, Alistair., ed. *The Scope of Political Theology.* London: SCM Press, 1978.

Keller, Catherine. *God and Power: Counter-Apocalyptic Journeys.* Minneapolis: Fortress Press, 2005.

________. *On the Mystery: Discerning Divinity in Process.* Minneapolis: Augsburg Fortress, 2008.

________. *Face of the Deep: A Theology of Becoming.* London and New York: Routledge, 2013.

________. *Political Theology of the Earth: Our Planetary Emergency and the Struggle for a New Public.* New York: Columbia University Press, 2018.

Keller, Catherine, Nausner Michael and Rivera, Mayra, eds. *Postcolonial Theologies: Divinity and Empire.* St. Louis, Missouri: Chalice Press, 2004.

Keller Catherine and Laurel C. Schneider Laurel C., eds. *Polydoxy, Theology of Multiplicity and Relation.* London and New York: Routledge, 2011.

Landry Donna, MacLean Gerard, eds. *The Spivak Reader: Selected Works of Gayatri Chakravorty Spivak.* New York: Routledge, 1996.

Levinas, Immanuel. *Totality and Infinity, An Essay on Exteriority.* Trans. Alphonso Lingis. Pittsburg: Duquesne University Press, 1969.

Ludden, David, ed. *Reading Subaltern Studies.* Delhi: Permanent Black, 2001.

Magun, Artemy, ed. *Politics of the One: Concepts of the One and the Many in Contemporary Thought.* New York London: Bloomsbury, 2013.

Marion, Jean-Luc. *God without Being.* Chicago: Chicago University Press, 1991.

Mark, Sanders. *Gayatri Chakravorty Spivak, Live Theory.* London and New York: Continuum, 2006.

Massey, James. *Dr. B. R. Ambedkar: A Stud in Just Society*, New Delhi: Center for Dalit/Subaltern Studies, 2003.

McFague, Sallie. *The Body of God: An Ecological Theology.* Minneapolis: Fortress Press, 1993.

Metz, Johann B. *Theology of the World.* New York: Herder and Herder, 1969.

Milbank, John. *Theology and Social Theory: Beyond Secular Reason.* Malden: Blackwell, 2006.

Moltmann, Jurgen. *On Human Dignity: Political Theology and Ethics.* London: SCM Press, 1984.

________. *Theology of Hope: On the Grounds and Implications of Christian Eschatology.* New York: Harper and Row, 1968.

________. *The Crucified God.* San Francisco: Harper & Row, 1974.

Moore S. D. and Rivera, eds. *Planetary Loves: Spivak, Postcoloniality and Theology.* New York: Fordham University Press, 2011.

Morris, Rosalind C., ed. *Can the Subaltern Speak? Reflections on the History of an Idea.* New York: Columbia University Press, 2010.

Morton, Stephen. *Gayatri Chakravorty Spivak: Ethics, Subalternity and the Critique of Postcolonial Reason.* London: Polity Press, 2007.

Omvedt, Gail. *Buddhism in India.* New Delhi: Sage Publications, 2003.

Pui-lan, Kwok and Don Compier H., eds. *Empire and Christian Tradition: New Readings of Classical Theologians.* Minneapolis: Fordham Press, 2007.

Rathore Akash S. and Verma A., eds. *B. R. Ambedkar: the Budha and his Dharma, A Critical Edition.* New Delhi: Oxford University Press, 2011.

Richard Horsley, Richard., ed. *Paul and Empire: Religion and Power in Roman Imperial Society.* Harrisburg, P.A: Trinity Press, 1997.

Rieger, Jeorg. *Christ and Empire: From Paul to Postcolonial Times.* Minneapolis: Fortress Press, 2007.

Rieger, Joerg and Pui-lan, Kwok. *Occupy Religion: Theology of the Multitude.* New York & UK: Rowan & Littlefield Publishers, 2012.

Rieger, Joerg and Waggoner, Edward., eds., *Religious Experience and New Materialism: Movement Matters.* New York: Palgrave Macmillan, 2016.

Rivera, Mayra. *The Touch of Transcendence: A Postcolonial Theology of God.* Louisville, London: Westminster John Knox, 2007.

Roudrigues, Valerian, ed. *The Essential Writings of B. R. Ambedkar.* New Delhi: Oxford University Press, 2002.

Ruether, Rosemary Radford. *Sexism and God-Talk: Toward a Feminist Theology.* Boston: Beacon Press, 1983.

Said, Edward. *Orientalism.* London: Routledge, 1978.

Schmitt, Carl. *Political Theology: Four Chapters on the Concept of Sovereignty*. Chicago: University of Chicago Press, 1985.

Schussler Elizabeth Fiorenza. *The Power of the Word: Scripture and the Rhetoric of Empire.* Minneapolis: Fortress Press, 2007.

Simmons, William Paul. *Human Rights Law and the Marginalized Other.* New York: Cambridge University Press, 2011.

Simons, Jon, eds. *Contemporary Critical Theorists: From Lacan to Said.* UK: Edinburgh University Press, 2004.

Smith, James K. A. *Introducing Radical Orthodoxy, Mapping a Post-Secular Theology.* Grand Rapids: Michigan: Baker Academic, 2004.

Spivak. *In other Worlds: Essays in Cultural Politics.* New York: Mithuen, 1987.

________. *The Postcolonial Critic: Interviews, Strategies, Dialogues.* New York: Routledge, 1990.

________. *The Spivak Reader: Selected Work of Gayatri Chakravorty Spivak.* Donna Landry and Gerald M. Maclean (eds.). New York & Routledge, 1998.

________. *A Critique of Postcolonial Reason: Toward a History of the Vanishing Present.* London: Cambridge, 2003.

________. *Death of Discipline.* New York: Columbia University Press, 2003.

________. *Other Asias.* Oxford: Blackwell, 2008.

Taylor, Mark C. *Erring: A Postmodern A/theology.* Chicago: University of Chicago Press, 1984.

Taylor, Mark Lewis. *The Theological and the Political, On the Weight of the World.* Minneapolis: Fortress Press, 2010.

Thomas, M. M. *A Diaconal Approach to Indian Ecclesiology*. Rome & Tiruvalla: CIIS & CSS, 1995.

Vries, Hent de and Sullivan, Lawrence E., eds. *Political Theologies: Public Religion in a Post-secular World.* Delhi: Orient Longman, 2006.

Vinayaraj, Y. T. *Dalit Theology after Continental Philosophy.* Switzerland: Palgrave Macmillan, 2016.

________. *Intercessions: Theology, Liturgy, and Politics.* New Delhi: ISPCK, 2016.

________. *Theology after Spivak.* New Delhi: ISPCK, 2016.

________. *Empire, Multitude, and the Church: Theology after Hardt and Negri.* New Delhi: ISPCK, 2017.

________. *Church and Empire: Detailing Theological Musings.* New Delhi: Christian World Imprints, 2019.

________. *Faith in the Age of Empire: Christian Doctrines in a Postcolonial Sensibility.* Singapore & New Delhi: CWM/ISPCK, 2010.

Ward, Graham. *Christ and Culture.* London: John Wiley & Sons, 2008.

Williams, James. *Gilles Deleuze's Difference and Repetition: A Critical Introduction and Guide.* Delhi: Motilal Banarsidas Publishers, 2008.

Zelliot, Eleanor. *Ambedkar's World: The Making of Babasaheb and the Dalit Movement.* Delhi: Navayana, 2004.

Zene, Cosimo, ed. *The Political Philosophies of Antonio Gramsci and B. R. Ambedkar: Itineraries of Dalits and Subalterns.* London & New York: Routledge, 2013.

Zizek, Slavoj and Milbank, John. *The Monstrosity of Christ: Paradox or Dialectic?* Ed. Creston Davis. Cambridge: MIT Press, 2009.